THE TEN COMMANDMENTS OF PROPAGANDA

THE TEN COMMANDMENTS

OF PROPAGANDA

by

BRIAN ANSE PATRICK

ARKTOS
LONDON 2012

First electronic edition published in 2011 by Goatpower Publishing.

First printed edition published in 2013 by Arktos Media Ltd.

Copyright © 2013 by Brian Anse Patrick/Goatpower Publishing.

Printed in the United Kingdom.

ISBN **978-1-907166-81-5**

BIC classification:
Political campaigning and advertising (JPVL)
Communication studies (GTC)
Media, information and communication industries (KNT)

Editor: Tobias Ridderstråle
Cover Design: Andreas Nilsson
Layout: Daniel Friberg

Cover and interior photographs: Tom Osswald
Model: Brooke Wagner

ARKTOS MEDIA LTD
www.arktos.com

Fodder for your mind

TABLE OF CONTENTS

INTRODUCTION

You have already been worked in a subtle way. How? Although the title of this book is *The Ten Commandments of Propaganda*, you will actually find eleven commandments here, and much other information beside.

The reference to the Ten Commandments accesses something already stored in your brain, waiting. The title calls and activates it with virtually no effort on your part. In an instant you already understand pretty much the whole drift of a fairly complicated concept that I am proposing. You know that you have encountered a set of precepts, *shalts* and *shalt-nots,* designed to guide thought and behavior. And by merely understanding all this, you are now well on the way to being persuaded of what I will have to say, for to understand is perhaps halfway to being persuaded. My task would be much more difficult if I had to assemble this whole idea from basic elements. Simply put, for any propaganda to be effective as mass persuasion, it must somehow resonate with ideas that are already in people's heads. To do otherwise is to attempt an entirely new installation of ideas and concepts, which requires far too much work on your part. So I have done the work for you, a sort of cognitive pre-packaging that takes advantage of the human propensity for avoiding work.

But don't mistake propaganda for a mere set of tricks. Nor am I trying to propagandize you at the moment, just trying to demonstrate a technique that I hope will draw your interest. I am acting within my role as a professor who has been intensely interested in propaganda for many years, and while professors (and writers) have quite often been propagandists for various causes, good and evil, wittingly and unwittingly, what I attempt here is merely to share a set of principles codified in the course of teaching and research. I do here what professors are supposed to do in an ideal world, which is to profess what they believe to be true and useful based on judgment, experience (real world and academic) and familiarity with a wide and deep body of well-vetted work that has been produced on their topic of specialization. One might say this is *education* — beware, though, because education has, as often as not, conveyed a great deal of propaganda, and highly educated people tend to be more, not less, susceptible to propaganda than are the uneducated.[1] However, I prefer to think of my effort here as a continuation of a *conversation* that has been ongoing for many years in western culture. You may at some point wish to participate in this conversation.

Also, more pragmatically, you may quite likely find this book useful for both offense and defense in your personal and professional life. You may imagine yourself unaffected by propaganda, but the person who thinks himself above propaganda is quite possibly its creature.[2]

---

1   Contrary to educated opinion, the highly educated are generally more susceptible to propaganda than others because they live, probably more than others, in a stream of symbols and information that come to wholly inform their beliefs about the world. On this see that great work by the French philosopher of propaganda Jacques Ellul, perhaps the most profound commentator on the subject: Jacques Ellul, *Propaganda: The Formation of Men's Attitudes* (New York: Alfred A. Knopf, 1965). Ellul regarded propaganda as necessary for individual social adjustment to the modern mass society, such that many people become psychologically and spiritually "crystallized" by propagandas. This is a tragedy because not only do people become entirely creatures of propaganda, their capacity for inner development is also blighted; in other words they stop growing. Viewed this way, propaganda is serious business, even more so if one believes in an afterlife because it causes a person to waste limited time and infinite potential. Interestingly, people who are not members of a mass society, who belong to traditional, more or less self-dependent organic groups or cultures, are difficult or impossible to propagandize because they already understand the world on their own terms. This is one of the reasons why totalitarian dictators such as Stalin resorted to killing or dispersing them — by the millions at times, e.g. the Kulaks — because they were resistant to management by state propaganda. There is, though, a special type of propaganda that Ellul thought more effective on the uneducated, namely *agitprop*, shorthand for *agitation propaganda*.

2   A frequently alleged goal of higher education is to impart critical thinking skills. This implies an attainment of some elevated level of objectivity and logical detachment.

So here is my method. Although propaganda is an immense modern undertaking, I have tried to keep the text short and readable. After this introduction, in which I will attempt a synopsis of propaganda's arrival on the modern scene, I will move right on to the Commandments. Commentary, references and those "illuminating" digressions to which academics are prone are consigned to footnotes and appendices, some of which are self-contained essays in their own right. The purpose here is to promote readability without sacrificing depth or technical correctness. The footnotes will not only direct interested readers to other sources, but will show the interconnectedness of propaganda with social and administrative sciences and with other fields; for there is no getting away from propaganda. Any preaching on my part will also be confined to footnotes. The footnotes also summarize and comment on significant books, research papers, and their authors, including a few classic propaganda films (which I encourage you to watch online so as to better understand these "timeless" principles). The footnotes themselves provide a fairly good overview of history, research, and techniques of propaganda — especially within propaganda's social-scientific sister disciplines; for a great deal of social science, theory and method, especially social psychology, has been linked quite directly with improving or discovering mechanisms of propaganda. For example, survey research, now a universal practice, was essentially brought into widespread service in order to measure susceptibilities and effects of propaganda on target populations.[3]

Listening to colleagues who teach "critical thinking skills," however, I find that the ideology of the teacher tends to dictate the direction of any "critical" thinking. For example, the liberal Democrat chooses to dissect the political rhetoric of the conservative Republican, showing it as lacking in logical integrity, mere "propaganda;" while the conservative Republican dissects the "propaganda" of the liberal Democrat, showing it to be emotional, vague drivel. Both analysts, however, are themselves creatures of propaganda (and they are probably both right in their analysis, they just need to apply the missing half of it upon themselves). How often the cutting edge of critical thinking seems so directed away from the self! This is also a fault of many of the current websites and books that purport to analyze propaganda. Incidentally, the word "creatures" in the context as it is used in this book means a "creation of," for example, as in "God's creatures."

3 I do not take very seriously the self-promotional notion put forward by pollsters that through polls/surveys a more perfect democracy might be obtained by better representing people's needs and desires. The practical use of survey data is often merely to take advantage of needs, credulities and weaknesses to design a product or candidate that people will "buy" given the exigencies of the times. There is little difference in this regard between marketing candidates and selling personal grooming products. I am definitely not saying that polls and surveys are ineffective tools in modern mass

Each Commandment has its own chapter, although each can be applied in many ways, as befits general principles. The Commandments are simple, but have ramifying applications that will be suggested by using straightforward examples. This may sometimes lead to a bit of overlap between the Commandments in their applications, but each Commandment as an action-principle nonetheless remains distinct. I will often employ extreme examples because they more clearly illustrate principles.

Just as it is by no means the first, this book cannot in any sense be the last word on propaganda. This field of endeavor is too big, too specialized, too pressing and too ongoing for such a book to even exist. Propaganda has become one of the grand undertakings of modernity. Without it there could be no bureaucratic-corporate organizations or states, mass democratic or otherwise, for just as humans are characterized by the ability to communicate with each other, modern bureaucratic administrative organizations are characterized by a reliance on propaganda, both externally and internally. Propaganda is a chief means by which the organizations that dominate modern life try to communicate power.[4]

Propaganda as a Situation

More than a mere set of techniques, propaganda is situational in nature. It is an organized bid for the right to interpret meaning in a given set of circumstances. The really big propagandas seek interpretive monopoly

society, but the benefits of their effectiveness seem to accrue mainly to their sponsors, and not their targets, although the sponsors have many ethical rationales worked out on how these data allow them to serve their audiences better. A perhaps more realistic analogy: a survey functions like a bombsight that helps to hit a target. Many surveys are proprietary, undertaken for example by political parties, and are used to inform the daily evasion- and escape-type maneuvers of political figures.

4   Harold D. Lasswell, whom I regard as the Original Big Daddy of propaganda research, observed: (1) propaganda is but one of three social management tools universally used by elites, the other two being violence and economic (dis)incentives. However, propaganda is often the most cost-effective and efficient tool because it can be undertaken at relatively little cost or risk and, if properly installed, the beliefs and behaviors of the person affected are programmed for the foreseeable future; (2) when propaganda is directed outside of an organization it is often called *public relations*, and; (3) when propaganda is directed within an organization it is often called *human relations* or *human resource management*. Here I have very roughly paraphrased him. I highly recommend his *Propaganda Technique in the World War* (New York: Knopf, 1927).

over the things that matter most. They are totalitarian in scope, e.g., religion, mass politics and social movements often seek to impose interpretations on the meaning of human existence, including its history, future, social relations, property, in short, aiming at the regulation of life itself. Propagandas also occur on a much smaller scale as everyday attempts to monopolize or control meaning in local, more confined situations where there exist domains and resources worth contesting, e.g., school, district or college administrators who serve out highly selective interpretations of reality so as to reinforce power, position and authority. Hence, propaganda scholar Jacques Ellul's wonderful remark that everything is explained thanks to propaganda. The benefits of these explanations, however, mostly accrue to their makers.

Many definitions of propaganda have been suggested.[5] Some are dramatic, some banal, some arcane, some narrow (there are many subtypes and techniques), and a few, downright obtuse. One of the more useful belongs to Walter Lippmann, who as a staffer in the Woodrow Wilson presidential administration saw firsthand the advent of modern American propaganda in the First World War. Lippmann viewed propaganda as inevitable in today's mass democracies, where voters are far removed physically and perceptually from political events, and must therefore rely on interpretive experts to inform their citizenship. We call it propaganda, said Lippmann, when a group of people who control access to some event releases information about it in such a way as to benefit themselves.[6] Notice that this implies both organization and self-interested interpretation of the meaning of reality.

A common misperception is that propaganda makers are necessarily the creatures of an ideology, culture or belief system, and their propaganda is primarily intended as a vehicle to disseminate these beliefs. While this is sometimes true, the situational view of propaganda suggests otherwise: in general, propaganda-making elites say and do what needs to be said and done to advance or maintain themselves and their organization. That they may also convince themselves with their own propaganda is beside the point. Their ideologies, as well as their actions, tend to be dictated by pragmatism and a will for power. While many people may see this pseudomorphic tendency as

---

5   See Appendix One.
6   Lippmann's *Public Opinion* (New York: Harcourt Brace & Co., 1922).

a character defect,[7] it accounts for the legendary slipperiness of politicians and bureaucrats; it may also be their chief survival skill.

Propaganda's antecedent, *persuasion*, dates to before Aristotle's time, back when it was known simply as *rhetoric*. However, in modern times, the idea of rhetoric, which Aristotle formulated as an ethical and logical tool for arriving at truth through reasoned debate in face-to-face settings, has degenerated, more or less, into merely a set of tricks used to inform advertising and mass and organizational propagandas.[8] "Rhetoric," accordingly, has acquired negative connotations as the term crops up in everyday speech,[9] while *mass persuasion* is merely a euphemism for propaganda.

I complete this introduction with a brief comprehensive history of propaganda. As an academic, I regard such a foundation as useful

---

7   My own impression is that this trait is innate to politicians and to some extent to any effective leader. Recall that epithets often attached to Homer's Odysseus depict him as wily, clever in speech and well spoken, crafty, of many devices, although often he is an outright prevaricator. But thus he prevails. Elisabeth Noelle Neumann, a German public opinion survey researcher, speculated that people — especially politicians — have a "quasi-statistical organ" that senses even small changes in the winds of public opinion and allows for appropriate personal adjustments in accord with the changing direction of the herd. Fear of isolation controls people in her view. She calls her theory "The Spiral of Silence" for its tendency to shut down minority opinions.

8   A former journalist and speechwriter acquaintance praises Aristotle's *Rhetoric* as, "The best book on corporate communication ever written." I often have required students to read *Rhetoric* for classes on persuasion, propaganda and public presentations. Aristotle placed rhetoric, which he defined as the art of finding the available means of persuasion in any set of circumstances, on a scientific and ethical foundation. He was the first and quite possibly the best to treat the subject in this way.

9   An exception to my remark is the current academic study of rhetoric, a somewhat moldering discipline preserved in a few university departments here and there. Rhetoricians study lexical techniques and devices, argumentation, and may even read Cicero. Aristotle is also part of the canon, although I have met or read few who seem to understand him, a notable exception being rhetorician Kenneth Burke, who is drier than dust. These modern rhetoricians tend toward the pedantic, however. They seem to make little impression on modern discourse when applying their discipline. It is a more or less backward-looking undertaking: they can tell you retrospectively why something worked, but cannot plot anything new. I've never met one who could write a good speech, they can only tell you why some past speech was good. An exception among rhetorician-scholars is J. Michael Sproule, who has written perhaps as lucidly as anyone on propaganda, and who has maintained that the practice of true rhetoric can revitalize democracy. I highly recommend Sproule's works on propaganda — especially his article "Progressive Propaganda Critics and the Magic Bullet Myth" (*Critical Studies in Mass Communication*, Vol. 6, No. 3) in which he reviews how the propaganda analysis era of the 1920s-1930s is not only misremembered and mistaught in many university communication classes, but also how Marxist-derived critical theorists have blotted out the sun in many university departments (my words, not his).

in obtaining a complete understanding. But the reader who is mainly interested in practical application may well think otherwise and move directly on to the Commandments. You are in command.

Three Waves of Propaganda

Propaganda can be thought of as having arrived in a progressive series of waves, each surging higher than the last. From the beginning, it has been the intimate companion of bureaucracy. The first wave originates in the early seventeenth century when Pope Gregory XV established the *Congregatio de Propaganda Fide*, the Congregation for the Propagation of the Faith, as an official department or ministry of the Roman Catholic Church. The Congregation was undoubtedly the first global communication/propaganda campaign and became, over time, so powerful that the cardinal in charge came to be called the Red Pope. Its scope included just about everything that had to do with propagation of organizational growth and uniformity of thought under Catholicism, in the Old and the New World, including the establishment of national colleges for the education of priests, and missions to foreign nations.[10] Owing to this ecclesiastical origin, it was not until perhaps 100 years ago that the term propaganda crept into everyday language in the sense used today to connote informational manipulation in mass secular politics. Had someone been called a "propagandist" back in the seventeenth or eighteenth centuries, however, it very likely would have been taken as a reference to a Jesuit priest.

Propaganda was created in large part as a weapon against heretics, unbelievers and reformers as personified in Martin Luther and others, who had successfully challenged the interpretive monopoly that the Church had maintained for centuries regarding the meaning and conduct of life in Western Europe. This monopoly had not been confined to the "merely" spiritual. God ruled Heaven and Earth and the "one true Church" effectively controlled access to God by means of

---

10 The Congregation was a complicated organizational undertaking. My simplification here does it no justice. It had a number of other functions concerning the organization of parishes and canon law. A discussion of some of its ways and means can be found in Richard A. Viguerie and David Franke's *America's Right Turn*. (Chicago: Bonus Books, 2004).

a policy that reserved the reading and interpretation of scripture, as well as the retail dispensation of Divine Grace via the sacraments, to Church officials: an unauthorized interpretation was "heresy," punishable by death.

The Church functioned as God's exclusive agent, so it said, and was willing to back up this claim by any means necessary. It tolerated no competition. The Reformation amounted to a rejection of this monopoly and the ecclesiastical bureaucracy that ran it. Protestants won the right to interpret absolute reality as they deemed it to be represented in scripture, thereby cutting out these middlemen.

Please do not be misled into thinking that I am trying to beat up religion. I merely describe an *informational sociology* that benefited an elite, well-organized group. This is the situation of propaganda, an entirely earthly phenomenon. By means of this first world ministry of propaganda the Church attempted to re-impose informational dominance in new and improved form, i.e., it sought global uniformity of thought. For an example of the spirit in which this effort was undertaken, Ignatius Loyola, founder of the Jesuits — the shock troops of this campaign — wrote: "To arrive at the truth in all things, we ought always to be ready to believe that what seems to us white is black, if the hierarchal Church so defines it."

The Congregation for the Propagation of the Faith was very successful, which explains, for instance, why much of the New World became and remains Catholic. But the Church never regained control over Northern Europe's Protestants or the Enlightenment Age philosophers — who went on to set up or influence new informational sociologies (some of which eventually amalgamated to become the United States of America).

It is no coincidence that the origin of *propaganda* is coupled to another concept that defines the modern era — *bureaucracy*. When sociologist Max Weber described the emergence and characteristics of the rational scientific organization called bureaucracy, he used the Roman Catholic Church as a model. The Congregation for the Propagation of the Faith was itself a model bureaucracy, with its many departments, protocols, reporting channels and national branches. So in these two vital areas — propaganda and bureaucracy — the Church's stamp upon modern secular life may prove even more enduringly pervasive than its spiritual one.

Second Wave

A second wave coincides with the First World War and its immediate aftermath. Talent, knowledge, new forms of mass media, communication technologies, governmental bureaucracy, need and circumstance all converged to establish a set of enduring practices. Viewed from the U.S. perspective, beginning in 1914, British propagandists first directed their considerable ingenuity toward dragging America into the war. They used publicity techniques and social influence directed at American opinion leaders to inundate the U.S. with atrocity stories and accounts sympathetic to the brave Allies and helpless Belgium, across which the Germans had tromped. Belgium was sometimes portrayed as a maiden violated by a Kaiser-like gorilla, identifiable by a Prussian military uniform with its ridiculously pointed *Pickelhaube* helmet (propaganda technique has relied much on heavy-handed stereotypes of this sort).

The British achieved a brilliantly simple mastery of the American informational sociology. Early on in the war, the British Navy cut the transatlantic cable from Germany, assuring henceforth that the great majority of war news going to America originated in Britain.[11] The modern, popular use of the term *propaganda* as a pejorative and synonym for deceptive communication emerges about this time, but British and, later, American propagandists firmly linked its use with the Germans.

Upon entering the war officially in 1917 (it had already been supplying Britain with food, materials and munitions) America established an organization that set the pattern for professional propagandists ever since: the Committee on Public Information ("CPI"). CPI has been called "America's first propaganda ministry."[12] CPI created

---

11 The Germans did not help themselves by conducting a klutzy logic-based campaign to explain the war to Americans. While the Germans were making highly technical legalistic arguments and placing modest newspaper advertisements warning Americans not to sail on the doomed *Lusitania* and other transatlantic liners, the British were dominating the U.S. information system, decrying the destruction of Christian civilization by the mad, pagan Hohenzollerns (Prussian royalty) who skulked in submarines to better spring upon and murder women and children. Much of this material appears crude to modern media-savvy audiences, but was entirely appropriate to audiences of that time, and would probably work again under the right circumstances.

12 See especially "America's First Propaganda Ministry: The Committee on Public Information During the Great War" by Robert Jackall and Janice Hirota in *Propaganda* edited by R. Jackall (New York: New York University Press, 1995).

massive public support for the war effort, despite a strong American isolationist tradition to stay out of "entangling" European alliances and wars. CPI quickly achieved near total interpretive dominance regarding the meaning of the War for Americans. In addition to providing newspapers with wholesome, staged photographs of the "boys" conscripted into military service and regular pre-written news articles on the war effort (nowadays called *press releases*), terms like *morale, public opinion* and, of course, *public information* were used to describe CPI's activities.

Total war begat total propaganda. Or perhaps it was the other way around — for total propaganda made total war into a moral obligation — i.e., it is one thing to conduct a limited war for strategic purposes, e.g., oil, and quite another to battle on behalf of Christian civilization. Few if any photographs of the four-million-plus military dead on the Allies' side ever appeared in any American or British newspaper.[13] This too was no accident. The war was so bloody and industrialized that some military professionals referred to the front lines as the "sausage factory" — fresh, identifiable cuts of meat in, sausage out.[14] The propagandists, however, focused on the glory and chivalric righteousness of the struggle.

In America, while CPI's energetic director, George Creel, publicly eschewed censorship, CPI was distributing voluntary media guidelines that had more moral force than any mere government decree. CPI's 75,000 "four minute men," all civilian volunteers, spoke at local theaters on the talking points of the week, addressing a cumulative audience of more than 300 million individuals in the course of the war. Creel mobilized dramatists, college professors and students, authors, advertising professionals, film makers and artists — e.g., Charles Dana Gibson, creator of the "Gibson Girl," and a CPI Division of Pictorial Publicity produced posters, an important mass medium in that pretelevision age. Many perhaps seem corny by today's standards, e.g., "The United States Army Builds Men," which highlighted the crafts,

---

13 In these days when newscasts and advertising use the same words to describe a new variety of bubble gum that saints once used to describe religious experiences, words often fail to describe phenomena meaningfully. Therefore, to say the war inflicted horrible carnage often means little to modern sensibilities, hence the illustrations in Appendix Two.

14 See Appendix Two for background on war horrors as recorded by Ernst Jünger's WWI narrative based on his diaries, *Storm of Steel*, which conveys some idea of the corpse-reek of the trenches.

character (depicted by a mail-clad knight) and physique that one could acquire by signing up. But much the same bait informs today's television recruiting ads, albeit upgraded by modern cinematographic technique. Creel underscored the importance of the "battle of the fences," upon which the posters were hung. CPI was so successful that things German became anathema for a time in America — including German philosophy, music, surnames and the language itself. Picking up on themes in British propaganda, the Germans were characterized as murderers, nun-rapists and killers of babies — an atrocity attributed to the Germans was the game of bayonet catch played with babies.[15]

Possibly, the only really clear and enduring outcome of that "war to end all wars" was to lodge the idea of propaganda into the American consciousness. Later the American propagandists bragged, however, and it became quite apparent the Germans had not been the only propagandists, nor in fact had they been even particularly good propagandists. Creel published on how CPI "advertised" the war — a euphemism he evidently preferred over "propaganda." He rationalized CPI's manifold activities as the "battle for men's minds" and the "gospel of Americanism," which was spread not only within America, to both foreign and native-born via appropriate media and social channels, but also in Europe, Russia and Asia by means of American "news services."

When Congress curtailed CPI activities at war's end, former CPI functionaries began to apply their propagandistic skills on behalf of commercial interests. Thus was born the "industry" of public relations. Ed Bernays, a vivid example and regarded now as an iconic figure, appears to have invented the term *public relations* and taught the first university class on the subject. Using the terms *propaganda* and *public relations* interchangeably, he excelled at making "news" that furthered his employers' interests. He coined phrases such as "the engineering of consent" to describe this new science.[16]

---

15 See Appendix Three for a more detailed discussion of the virulence of some of these propaganda campaigns.

16 Among his other propaganda triumphs, while working for the American Tobacco Company, Ed Bernays was credited with creating a new mass market of women cigarette smokers simply by talking debutants into smoking cigarettes to symbolize women's freedom while they walked in the New York City Easter Parade. This artifice was covered in news worldwide, not as an artifice, but as a genuinely organic social event; respectable women subsequently began smoking in public — previously taboo, but suddenly high fashion. See Bernay's *Propaganda* (New York: Horace Liveright, 1928).

Also in this second wave period was launched the academic-scientific study of propaganda. At University of Chicago, Harold Lasswell wrote a seminal dissertation on propaganda technique in the World War, a field of endeavor that was eventually repackaged into the study of *communication*. Lippmann, progressing from propagandist to social commentator, published his famous *Public Opinion*, in which he pondered the problem of how to protect citizens from the mass opinion manufacturers. Concepts such as *attitudes, public opinion, psychology* and *stereotypes* were popularized. By the early 1920s Adolf Hitler was codifying his observations on military and mass movement propagandas that constitute perhaps the only sensible chapters in *Mein Kampf*.[17]

Lest the reader begin to think that I am merely stirring through the historical dust, all of these lines of inquiry remain sharply relevant today. For example, Lasswell's recipe, "How the enemy is to be treated in time of war," describes recent U.S. government information strategies in the Gulf War and the Iraq War to the point of being uncanny.[18] Hitler, in turn, extolled (although by no means invented) the principles of simplicity and repetition that underlie much of modern mass consumerism and advertising. Synthetic news techniques of the sort pioneered by Bernays and others now create most of the daily U.S. news stream; and although today's political communication scholars refer to these deceits as *pseudo-events*, they are real enough in their

---

17 Hitler regarded the masses as effeminate in nature and therefore vulnerable to crude emotional appeals. Acknowledging the effectiveness of the WWI British propagandists for their skill in demoralizing his countrymen, Hitler believed that Germany had been defeated more by propaganda and internal division exacerbated by propaganda than by mere strength of arms.

18 Lasswell writes in *Propaganda Technique and the World War:*
    "The identification of a particular foreign nation as the enemy may be established by three lines of inference. It invariably mobilizes first in the days of crisis (either openly or secretly) and commits acts of war, and by doing so, reveals a criminal anxiety to press matters to a finish. More than that, it invariably incriminates itself by endeavoring to maneuver our government into the position of an aggressor during the feverish negotiations preceding the final break. Behind all this, there invariably stands a record of lawlessness, violence and malice, which offers unassailable proof of a deliberate attempt to maim or destroy us." (p. 50)
    "So great are the psychological resistances to war in modern nations that every war must appear to be a war of defense against a menacing, murderous aggressor. There must be no ambiguity about whom the public is to hate. The war must not be due to a world system of conducting international affairs, nor to the stupidity or malevolence of all governing classes, but to the rapacity of the enemy. Guilt and guilelessness must be assessed geographically, and all the guilt must be on the other side of the frontier. If the propagandist is to mobilize the hate of the people, he must see to it that everything is circulated which establishes the guilt of the enemy." (p. 47)

own way because they provide the only representations of political reality that most people will ever know.[19] In these ways and others, bureaucratically-generated interpretations of reality overshadow virtually all other forms of social growth — e.g., in education, government and policy, and are announced and disseminated virtually in an ecclesiastical, top-down fashion.

In any case, by the 1920s it became obvious to many that wartime propaganda had poisoned the information well of American rational democracy. Indignation over this outrage continued until the World War II era. A prophylaxis attempted in the 1930s was the Institute for Propaganda Analysis, which among other activities, taught courses on propaganda in more than 500 American high schools. IPA's touchingly naïve "ABC's of Propaganda" and "Seven Devices of Propaganda" were intended to protect innocents against the evils of special interest communications. The "devices" included *glittering generalities*, e.g., use of virtue words such as "justice" and "freedom" without any clear definition or meaning, and *card-stacking*, to indicate tendentiously manipulated arguments building toward a foregone conclusion.

The Third Wave

The general mobilization of U.S. society in World War II signaled the end of such well-intentioned muddling. A whole generation of social scientists, often with government sponsorship, began to conduct research on how to do better, more effective propaganda. Some of the many areas explored included message design, credibility factors, inoculation against enemy propaganda, communication campaigns, communication effects derived from the manipulation of different variables, authority/ obedience, content analysis (a way of quantifying communication content so trends and sources can be identified and propaganda measured) and the use of small groups (e.g., *group dynamics*) to change attitudes,

---

19 Journalists and news organizations rely heavily on pseudo-events and press releases. Propagandists and PR professionals are well aware of this. Please forgive the following rather farmerly metaphor, but one could view the U.S. news information system as a sort of trough into which propagandists, calling themselves PR professionals, regularly dump information; journalists and news organizations nose in hog-like to feed at the trough. The notion of an independent and objective news system conducted by truth-seeking journalists is highly romanticized, exaggerated and self-serving in regard to the actual role of mass media journalists in interpreting reality.

and, especially, behaviors, through the means of normative group pressure. This latter so-called "horizontal propaganda" conducted by means of the small group has since become the trend in social and corporate management practice; it tightens controls over employees while creating the illusion of democracy, a very advanced technique. Today there is more social science of this sort being taught in modern business schools than in university social science departments, so one might well wonder if U.S. society ever truly demobilized after the Second World War, when propaganda emerged as its social norm.

The Third Wave also produced or inspired volumes of social scientific research with direct applications to propaganda, inaugurating a golden age of behavioral studies that lasted until the 1960s or so. Perhaps the most memorable was Stanley Milgram's series of obedience to authority experiments. Milgram showed that under the guise of a "learning experiment," approximately 50 percent of workaday, average people would repeatedly administer 450-volt electric shocks to a restrained person. They would continue despite screams and demands for release, and even after the restrained person became non-responsive and quite possibly dead or unconscious. Although the experiment was rigged — no shocks were actually delivered, screams were pre-recorded, and the person supposedly being "shocked" was a confederate of the experimenters — the naïve subject who was giving the shocks did not know any of this. In effect, so I believe, Milgram synthesized the basic elements of mass murder/genocide in the laboratory — Nazified monsters were not necessarily an ingredient, just average people under a compelling set of circumstances.[20]

---

20 The shock experiment required no coercion: an anonymous authority figure clad in a white lab coat merely urged subjects on, e.g., "The experiment requires that you continue." No actual shocks were administered, but the subjects had no way of knowing this. Milgram himself seemed horrified at the compliance rate, noting that if a contrived laboratory experiment could so readily produce such behavior, then how much greater were the pressures toward conformity in real life situations, with their well-established authority figures and looming social expectations. Solomon Asch, for another famous example, showed convincingly that group pressure could distort a subject's perceptions of reality, e.g., his line experiment where subjects were "normed" into perceiving lines that were in actuality relatively short as being the longest in a set of lines.

Milgram made a movie called *Obedience* to demonstrate his experimental results. It is generally available online. It is often shown in psychology classes and is sometimes used as an example of an unethical research design that harms the subjects; some say subjects were traumatized because of the stress of the experiment, which resulted in laughing fits, nervous motions, grimacing, etc.; or that informed consent was somehow violated by the extent of the deception. I don't buy these

Ubiquity of Propaganda

Consider your own situation and behavior. Unless you happen to be reading this in a maximum-security prison, probably no armed guards oversee your activities. Instead you largely manage your own behavior based on ideas and expectations that have somehow found their way into your head. Education, training, socialization, information availability, habit and perception channel your actions in fairly predictable and productive ways, as far as the larger society is concerned. You are harnessed to something bigger than yourself. You quite possibly even imagine that you understand the larger world around you; which is perhaps a surer sign than any that some species of propaganda has taken hold.

Propaganda permeates modern mass-society democracy, which is based on nominal consent of the governed, and wherein coercion generally stands a safe remove in the background. Propaganda coordinates and connects mass democracy's human particles, assuring that many of them resonate on shared frequencies. Ellul believed that modern mass-man or woman needs propaganda as a matter of personal adjustment, necessary because of the relative meaninglessness of the individual in relationship to the mass. Propaganda answers questions of greater meaning that were once the province of religion, myth, tradition and organic community.[21] It orients, assures and even provides

---

claims, for the simple reason that people can and do rationalize away just about anything regarding their own behavior. My suspicion is that the experiment possibly did not affect its subjects enough.

21 *Mass Society Theory* underlies much thinking about propaganda and sociology. The newer "mass society" differs from the largely disappearing "traditional society" in that the mass individual stands "alone in the crowd." By this I indicate today's urbanized, relatively rootless, consumer/citizen, an alienated person who is sundered from traditional roles and values, who might be expected to go off and "find himself." The latter concept would have been ridiculous to most people in the past, who knew full well what and who they were.

Mass society theory begins to be well articulated with Gustav Le Bon's *The Crowd,* which attributes a heightened suggestibility to people in crowds and mobs, the kind of group experience most available to mass society members, who therefore become less rational and more animal-like in their needs and expressions. Hysteria and herd behaviors such as riots are basic attributes of crowds andmobs, who may in a moment turn from maudlin to homicidal. When the individual becomes bound up in a crowd, rationality is compromised. There is little doubt in my mind that Le Bon's writings influenced Hitler and many other propagandists. Much of the Nazi mass demonstration propaganda seems designed around the idea of the individual's heightened suggestibility in crowds, of being swept away in a grand march to the future.

an identity without having to go through all the work of building one's own. We have grown accustomed to its constant streaming — words-without-end-amen — much like listening to the radio or television provides an illusion of connection to the larger world when one is alone.

It wasn't always like this. Once upon a time propaganda was the exception. When Congress abruptly curtailed CPI activities at war's end in 1919, it left many wartime matters hanging unexplained in America, e.g., President Wilson's peace treaty. Creel, however, who had propagandized on a scale unprecedented, accepted the cessation of official propaganda without any apparent reservation. Creel wrote:

"Nothing would have been more instantly attacked, and justly attacked, than the use of governmental machinery and public funds for any such purpose. Bad as conditions are today, they would be infinitely worse had the President attempted to support his cause by "press-agenting" with the people's money. As for the Committee on Public Information, its duties ceased automatically when fighting ceased."[22]

So the man who bragged of directing the global distribution of more than 75 million pieces of print propaganda, according to CPI records, had moral reservations about the use of propaganda in peacetime by elected democratic representatives who would unethically benefit by it.

How things have changed! Not only do few people nowadays express any such reservations, it would appear that yet fewer even conceive that such reservations might be in order. Today the White House alone employs several hundred propagandists or technicians in propaganda, in war and peace, at horrifying public expense, "press-agenting" with the people's money every day of the year. None of these support people are *called* propagandists, however. I once worked on a presidential visit as an official of the host state. A White House representative and I did a walk-through of the prepared site. Behind the stage holding the bulletproof podium and the presidential seal, White House Communications personnel had set up a covered platform in an evergreen tree from which a technician would be operating the teleprompter. The representative lifted the canvas cover and said, "It's just

22 See George Creel's, *How We Advertised America* (New York: Harper, 1920). Also, "A New Device In War" in *Our Times: The United States 1900-1925, Vol. V, Over Here 1914-1918,* by M. Sullivan (New York: Charles Scribner's Sons, 1933).

like the Wizard of Oz: you pull back the curtain and there's a little guy operating the levers." We have become inured. I have often felt while trying to convey somewhat the scale of contemporary propaganda to today's mass media-bred students, that the task might be comparable to trying to explain the existence of water to a fish, a substance which constantly surrounds it, but of which it would quite likely be insensible. Much of what they seem to think they know about the world — fashion, music, current events, history — are but remnants of various propaganda/communication campaigns.

Not only has the public sector long been given over to the propagandists, so has much of the private corporate sector. Managerial elites use shareholder money, and, lately, public funds called bailouts and stimulus packages, to further the dodging of blame and taking of credit that sometimes seems to comprise their primary substantive expertise. Despite the ostensible business of these organizations, a main product seems to have transmogrified over time into propaganda, a process which organizational behaviorists call "goal displacement."[23] Corporate elites dominate the flow of information about their organizations in ways so as to confound even the most diligent inquiry. What shareholder or deadline-driven journalist has the time, energy and resources to conduct an independent investigation of a large, complicated corporate entity, private or public? Where even to begin? Informationally, the game always heavily favors insiders with direct access to events. British Prime Minister Lloyd George once said of the British War Department, which he had overseen in 1915-1918, "They

---

23 Organizational behaviorists have long been aware to this aspect of bureaucracy. The concept of "goal displacement" derives from the work of sociologist Robert Michels, known too for his formulation of "The Iron Law of Oligarchy" which describes how even in supposedly democratic organizations the leaders seize control of the communication systems and use them to their own advantage and to cement their power:

"The hierarchal aspect of the bureaucratic structure and the concentration of the means of communication at the top, make the power position of the leader impregnable. Thus information can be manipulated (distorted or withheld from members) and the whole communication network can be used against any potential rival. Above all, the leader, by the exercise of his functions, gradually acquires a specialized knowledge and political skills (making speeches, writing articles, etc.) which makes him irreplaceable to the organization." (p. 27, Nicos P. Mouzelis, *Organisation and Bureaucracy: An Analysis of Modern Theories* (Chicago: Aldine publishing, 1968))

Of course in any large modern organization the leader has speechwriters and publicity people who perform these functions.

kept three sets of figures: one to mislead the public, another to mislead the government, and a third to mislead themselves."[24]

The more complicated things become, the more difficult they are to explain, yet there is more need than ever for explanation, and accordingly more opportunities arise for propaganda's handy explanations. Plus propaganda is much like an arms race — those who don't do it put themselves at a disadvantage, so the pressure is always to escalate.

Truth, Untruth, Propagandists and the Public Good

Regarding the matter of truth, despite what has been said about atrocity stories, propaganda is not merely lies — although lies, rumors and disinformation have been used. But the lie is not a generally effective technique, despite the Nazis' famous notion about the "Big Lie" inspiring more belief than a small one. Overt lies, when detected, compromise the credibility of the propagandist; however, the propagandist can always use a front organization or "leaks" to outsource incredible claims while still preserving the appearance of probity. Thus Ellul noted, in propaganda truth pays. There is no need to risk the lie when copious information consisting of select facts, arbitrary, operational definitions and statistics create a cognitive deluge which overwhelms the victim, who becomes therefore even more dependent on interpretive expert-propagandists to explain what it all means.

Additionally many matters within the province of propaganda are beyond truth or untruth *per se*, e.g., images or symbols. How can a photograph or an image be untrue? Unless offered as doctored evidence, an image merely is what it is. It may evoke a response, or a response to it can be conditioned through repetition, or it can be "interpreted," hence, in part, its power, e.g. the golden arches, the hammer and sickle. This observation applies to slogans as well, which are often intentionally ambiguous so as to allow people to see in them whatever they need to see, e.g., "Change you can believe in," which means anything, everything or nothing depending on the perceiver's predispositions. Additionally, since the main thrust of propaganda has

---

24 This gem is from William Manchester's two-volume biography, *The Last Lion: Winston Spencer Churchill*, vol. 2: Alone, 1932-1940 (Boston: Little, Brown, 1988), p. 613.

to do with the interpretation of meaning, which more often than not is ultimately unknown or in dispute, especially concerning complicated social issues, who is to say what may be the "correct" meaning of any major part of the human experience? The propagandist steps into this void, presenting a plausible case, perhaps one based on the crudest circumstantial evidence, but one suitable for his audience and purposes.

Who are all these propagandists? There is a powerful stereotype of the cartoon propagandist. Many still associate propaganda with Hitler, a residual effect that attests to the power of the American and British propaganda machinery in the Second World War. Joseph Goebbels, Hitler's "minister of propaganda" was shown as a sort of crippled ridiculous dwarf (although no one was talking about FDR creaking about in his wheelchair). Propaganda was linked with the creation of Nazi automatons on a jackbooted and trench-coated goosestep through history.[25] The propagandist-as-buffoonery stereotype was resurrected in the Iraq War in the person of Baghdad Bob, a virtual auto-parody, whom Americans loved to ridicule when CNN carried his out-of-skew reports on the progress of the war. The buffoon stereotype also rode again in the "great-man" grotesqueries, the statues and monuments, of the Saddam Hussein regime. One might recollect the much-televised event when sundry persons identified as the Iraqi people pulled down the colossus of Hussein with much not-so-obtrusive help from the U.S. military. The same trick had been pulled off in the film *October,* which commemorated the tenth anniversary of the 1917 Bolshevik Revolution in Russia, where "the people" are shown pulling down a colossus representing the Czar. Such burlesque demonstrations downplay the effectiveness of propaganda.

Rather than the monsters and their stooges, which are convenient to have around (Osama bin Laden was so perfect in this regard that he could have been designed by the Disney Studios), on the whole propagandists are more or less low key; they prefer business attire to leather trenchcoats, and are embedded in their organizations as bureaucrats and administrators, mundane in appearance and operation. Titles under which they operate are legion: vice president of external relations, lobbyists, government relations, public information specialists, communication directors, media specialists, publicity, any number of

---

25 See Appendix Four for discussion of U.S. and British propaganda successes in painting the Nazis and Japanese as fools, deviants or subhumans.

variants on "public relations"[26] and whatever else circumstances may suggest. In 1913, the U.S. Congress designed a measure to ban use of publicity experts by U.S. government agencies, regarding this practice as unethical, and barred designated budget money for such use. The gross result was merely that job titles changed. No one now has any firm idea just how many propaganda functionaries work for government — federal, state or local — partly because many have nebulous job titles. Executives, for example, use their powers to attach functionaries to departments that would seem to have nothing to do with propaganda, e.g., a Midwestern governor hires a person whom some would call a "political handler" with high level experience in large national trade associations, and situates him in the state's department of natural resources, where his only apparent function is to promote the governor.

Is propaganda evil by definition, or does it convey social benefits? It has often been defended or minimized. Lasswell discounted its long-term influence by claiming America's various propagandas would cancel each other out in a free marketplace of competing propagandas. This of course assumes a free market. Lasswell's assumption possibly no longer holds in the face of modern interpretive near-monopolies, e.g., government and ownership centralization, or the "cornering the market" in key areas within the information sociology, e.g., education policy, or the decline of citizen-based voluntary associations that might act as alternate information sources, and the concordant proliferation of staff-run groups wherein small, top-down organizations claim to speak on behalf of all humanity.

Bernays boasted that propaganda had helped to make America great by promulgating new products, markets and ideas. Others say that good propaganda works for the "public interest" while bad propaganda advances "special interests." Beware this line of argument, however, because autocrats routinely, if not invariably, claim the collective good as their warrant of personal legitimation. Further, "special interests" may well be you or anyone else who doesn't go along with

---

26 Public Relations professionals may object and will resort to self-serving ethical formulations for defense, a common one being that they act as intermediaries who interpret their clients to the world and the world to their clients, thus assuring equitable adjustments and something called "two-way" flow of communication. Balderdash. PR professionals represent their employers' interests and would not be employed for long if they failed to do so. That they may simulate conversation is but a tactic to advance these interests.

a current administrative agenda. Another common argument is that having more available information gives people more choices, so propagandists are therefore just providing a public service. Maybe this is true, but when information is thus subsidized it tends to serve those who have subsidized it, as is the case with press releases and think tank reports. Plus, propaganda is not neatly distinguishable from information. Is there even such a thing as neutral information? For information doesn't just spontaneously appear in media — it serves some purpose. In any case, the lone individual is not up to the task of collecting raw data on world, national or even local events, and must depend on propaganda's interpretive experts to turn such data into information.

Some degree of propaganda may be good when viewed as a cost-benefit calculation, although we must always wonder who is doing the arithmetic. We might consider here the near universal belief among Americans of belonging to something called "the middle class," a pretense that is absurd on its face. If the belief is regarded as a socialization propaganda, however, which causes people to aspire and behave "correctly" according to cultural models, the belief assures that much unpleasant work continues to get done. Arguing the contrary, though, such a belief may have permanently injured many who don't know the difference between being a consumer and a citizen, and who haven't truly developed themselves because they imagine themselves as having already "arrived." It may also have damaged the nation by decreasing sustainable productivity and creating a false bubble of prosperity that appears recently to have burst.

Also, without propaganda societal unity might disappear. Extreme fragmentation might result. This was a fear of the Church as well, that without centralized control of meaning, the virtues of a higher, greater order might disappear and interpretive pluralism might degrade to the level where everyone merely strives against everyone else in a brutish Hobbesian fashion. Good or bad, however, propaganda is an omnipresent environmental fact. It seems impossible to imagine a mass society without it.

Is a Fourth Wave swelling over us now? Perhaps. It may be too early to say whether computer-mediated communications will be a boon to propagandists or, instead, to individual freedom. That people have more information than ever before may simply mean that they receive more highly customized propaganda. Or it could mean that online interpretive communities will be enabled, allowing people more independence in constructing social meaning. My own belief is that the Web is a godsend for propagandists as well as for autonomous interpretive communities; but with what long-term results I do not know.

Before commencing with the Commandments, let me add just this. Although informed by science, propaganda is an art. There are no magic buttons. Good. Were this so, human freedom would disappear. But even though no magic buttons may exist, there are many buttons to push, many techniques designed to push them and many functionaries and organizations devoted to the pushing of buttons. Propaganda draws upon a great body of empirical knowledge. The Commandments incorporate this knowledge. Still, pragmatism drives the making of propaganda, as do the apparently unchanging needs of the human animal, an animal that is both rational and primitively emotional. Propaganda adapts. It may be the closest thing available to a universal social lubricant; it has the additional advantage of being both recyclable and cheap to manufacture. You will find your own applications for this knowledge. But above all do not imagine yourself immune either from propaganda's effects, or if you work in a modern organization, from its necessity. Like any list of precepts, these commandments can serve either as a positive or a negative guide to behavior.

The First Commandment

CONTROL THE FLOW OF INFORMATION

Controlling the flow of information is the most important commandment of propaganda. It is often sufficient in itself to win. If a propagandist can strategically dominate the readily available information within a particular informational sociology, this could be in a nation or an organization, it greatly lessens the chance that competing explanations (and their explainers) can thrive in that environment. Other ideas and explanations might exist, but if they are ignored, confined to private fantasy, or to limited circulation within self-contained or marginalized groups — e.g., grumblings in the mail-room or the ghetto — they probably won't matter very much overall.

Plus, there is only so much room for coherent shared information within any one system or in any one person's head, otherwise things get too complex to follow. Those who control the flow of information are the ones most likely to arrive there "firstest with the mostest" and thus prevent other ideas from taking root or flourishing.

Propagandists control information flow in two basic ways. The first, which must be done, is by becoming a source or distributor of information. The second, which may be done, and which often complements the first, is through exclusion of undesirable or contrary information. These could be thought of as offense and defense, or positive and negative controls, and although the concepts are simple enough, there are innumerable variations on how these things are done, some obvious and direct, others subtle.

The Propagandist as Source

By this first way, the propagandist becomes a principal information source, an information node, creating or managing information and its many possible channels. To succeed, the propagandist floods the environment, or its key areas, with his own symbols and purposive information via whatever media systems are available, perhaps even introducing some new forms of media to the system, trying to overwhelm any other relevant or competing sources through sheer presence, e.g., creating news events, press releases, town hall meetings, scientific reports, op-ed pieces, white papers, direct mail appeals, talk show appearances, books (which when attributed to political or corporate celebrities are often ghostwritten), "framing" stories such that they promote organizational goals, promotional items, political demonstrations, think tanks, commissions, ad hoc community-based or grassroots groups, roundtables, task groups and committees, neighborhood canvassers, posters, badges, slogans, advertising (which is merely paying an agent to deliver your package of symbolism), acting as a clearinghouse, starting a newspaper, discussion group, blog, newsletters, causing or encouraging the creation of public events and spectacles, and so on. Of course in all cases the propagandist controls or initiates formats and agendas, e.g., by constituting committees with friendly, known faces, or by making sure the town hall meeting takes place in a controlled venue with properly filtered questions and questioners, all while appearing inclusive, fair and scrupulously informative, when the reality is anything but. Forgetting not that a propagandist is essentially a self-serving interpreter of meaning, whatever means by which interpretation can be accomplished are acceptable, e.g. transforming raw data into information. Propagandists have even commissioned novelists to write on desired topics or provided Hollywood screenwriters with script ideas to weave into popular entertainment shows. The term "raising awareness" is sometimes used to describe such practice.[27]

All this is done as strategically as possible in consideration of the nature of the informational sociology so that the information/education/communication most affects the target population(s) or specified sectors of it by delivering appropriate "content." It is not enough to say, "We will use media and get the message out." This would be as wasteful as it is ineffective. "Which media intended for whom?" is the key consideration. One must pick the route, the messenger and the message for the specific target audience(s). For example, if the propagandist wishes to alarm senior citizens into voting or behaving in a desired way, this might be accomplished by frightening them with economic analyses or public opinion poll results (designed and administered for this purpose or merely adapted from preexisting research) that suggest severe rationing of health care to the elderly will soon take place if the "other" party has its way: seniors will have to pay more of their hard-earned money for significantly less care. The message may be customized to appropriate interest groups: the American Association of Retired Persons, for example, would likely relay it to its 30 million or so members; to specific media that seniors tend to use, especially perhaps local small town papers and radio stations that are hungry for news to serve this large portion of their market; through direct mailings in key voting districts to lists of seniors assembled from voting registration records; to local retirement communities, churches, seniors' groups and centers perhaps via a speakers bureau type arrangement. One must not forget the talk shows or use of distinguished celebrity seniors as spokespersons. Themes and concerns voiced in the campaign would resonate with those discovered by conducting focus groups with seniors. Only the most vivid and action-provoking messages, tested on other focus groups, would be crafted into the campaign, based on real fears and reactions expressed by real seniors while under suitable facilitation.

One might even use "push polls" to further alarm and mobilize the seniors. These are pseudo-polls conducted by telephoning or direct

---

27 John Steinbeck's World War II novel *The Moon is Down* (New York: Viking Press, 1942) dealt with Nazi occupation in Europe and was accordingly banned in Nazi-occupied countries, where it was said to be popular among resistance fighters. More currently, the Entertainment Council distributes script outlines to screenwriters for the purpose of 'educating' the public on the dangers of guns and gun ownership.

mailing members of the target population under the guise of survey-
ing their opinions, and asking provocative questions designed instead
to infuriate them into action, which might be calling elected representatives, voting in a specific way, or sending money. For example,
the "interviewer" might begin by asking, "Do you agree or disagree
with Party X's proposal that would increase the cost of prescription
drugs for seniors on Medicaid by 300 percent?" Of course the pollsters already know the indignant negative answers that will be given
to this question, and to all the others that will be asked, too. After an
ersatz poll is conducted the propagandist may issue a press release to
add to the flow of information: e.g., "Latest poll finds 76 percent of
seniors oppose proposed program." Talk radio shows might pick up
the release, too.

One might even use old-fashioned "telephone trees" to reach the
target audience, where each senior called is asked to telephone ten
other seniors and relay the message, and so forth. Even "scientific"
journals and the sacred cow of "research" often become tools of propaganda by publishing favorable findings. The propagandizing organization merely sponsors and promotes the sort of research that is needed.

By such means and others the propagandist may dominate, for
practical purposes, virtually all channels or media systems of readily
available information, including perhaps some relatively arcane channels that connect to special audiences, e.g., ministers, university professors, activities directors of senior citizen centers, social workers and
teachers, who may then redistribute this information to their charges
under the guise of "education." Notions of euthanasia and rationed
health care might be promulgated as well, both of which are virtually
guaranteed to fuel debate and disconcert seniors, who are more aware
than most of the ticking of the clock.

The important point is that public information does not just appear
one fine morning after having spontaneously assembled itself. News
and information is crafted and aimed at a target. Whether created
or commandeered, it somehow benefits its manufacturers when it is
delivered via appropriate channels to where it will presumably have
the most effect. There is an art to this as well, but crude perseverance
often pays off, too. Propagandists even excel at harnessing their causes
to natural events, using them to show concerned responses to earth-
quakes, wholesale death in its various forms, disasters or hurricanes,
e.g., hurricanes Irene, Katrina and Sandy and recent African famines

have powered various organizational propagandas, making heroes out of bureaucrats, and helping politicians in blue suits to seem "presidential."

Of course personnel, energy, time and money are required to generate and manage information, which is why the average individual or casual local association is so often disadvantaged in this game, although they may win an occasional inning, often by improvising new techniques to which the more slowly moving institutions have not yet adapted. But adaptation happens relatively quickly when a technique is seen to work — thus one sees "grass roots" mobilization regularly simulated by organizations that are run from the top down, e.g., the largely chimerical Million Moms March against gun violence, or the national teen anti-smoking campaign known as "The Stand." Organizational informational sources tend to dominate in the long run. And because propaganda is pragmatic, when the social climate changes so do the propagandas, but not necessarily the propagandists.

Exclusion

The second basic way by which propagandists control the information flow is by the exclusion of competing, inconvenient informational sources and channels. This is often done simultaneously with the first, although sometimes it need not be done at all, or only in small measure, e.g., when there is no serious organized competition.

An extremely effective example of exclusion, with far-reaching consequences, was mentioned in the introduction — Britain's cutting of the transatlantic cable from Germany at the beginning of the Great War. This simple, direct action precluded Germany's ability to meaningfully take part in public discussion of the war underway at the time in American news, thereby helping bring America into the war on the British side. Before the cut, roughly half of the war-related news in *The New York Times* originated in Germany, the other half in Britain. Afterward about 95 percent was British. German ideas were no longer seen nor heard and therefore no longer mattered. Such a public opinion formation process is analogous to a trial where the accused is not present to offer any defense.[28]

---

28 See Lippmann and Mertz, "A Test of the News" in *New Republic*, August 4, 1920 (supplement), pp. 1-42.

This exclusion was complemented by a strong positive policy of Britain acting as the principal information source. The British created and released, via appropriate channels and formats, news andinformation that carried only its views on the meaning of the war, e.g., atrocity stories, the idea that the Germans were waging a war on Christianity and trying to restore paganism, stirring martial poems and human interest stories such as that of a heroic British nurse executed for aiding the escape of British prisoner from the Germans, while German nurses treated in exactly the same way by the French were ignored (nor did the Germans know how to emotionally exploit this situation). News on the war became at every turn an indictment of Germany and sympathetic to the heroic British and their allies. Thus, exclusion helped ensure America's entry into the war, which resulted in a British victory that would have been most unlikely otherwise.

Exclusion, of which censorship is just another form, may be understood as being the reverse side of the propaganda coin. The very idea of censorship carries negative connotations, people become indignant at the notion, but this assumes that it is recognized as such. Often it is not. It is most unlikely that millions of readers of American newspapers ever realized how thoroughly sieved their information was during the First World War, or in other similar circumstances. A more modern parallel: you might ask yourself whence comes the news that you see and hear daily — and also from where it does not. Many important events occur every day, but relatively few are reported. Who are the originators of the news, or its gatekeepers? I bet you don't really know. Consumers of news — you, me, people in a hurry, people with jobs and real life concerns, students — seldom have the leisure to ponder such potentially troubling questions or follow them through, if asked. They are distant from events and must depend on second and third hand information, which gives propagandists many opportunities to intercept and sort through information. Another example, by what process was the information package assembled that you encountered in the form of your high school or college history book? Who selected what you now think of as history, and for what ideological or institutional purposes? You may be more vulnerable to information control than you may imagine. My guess is this may be the first time you considered its implications.

Ignoring unwelcome information is often a sound exclusionary tactic. I call this the *Harvard Technique*, although it was by no means invented at or limited to Harvard University, but because it has been popular there through the years.[29] This technique especially works if the unwelcome explainers lack resources, access to media or social prestige to make their ideas felt: the old and prestigious simply keep the new and less prestigious outside in the cold. For why dignify an unwelcome idea by admitting that it exists? This might imply that it deserves a response. Further, why waste bandwidth in one's own propaganda channels by needlessly acknowledging someone else's information? Let them try to find their own channels. Seeing that the good channels are usually "occupied," so to speak, or require considerable resources to enter, this alone may daunt any challenger. Responding to contrary ideas is done often only to seem fair-minded or to score points by beating up the arguments of opponents in such a way as to show the propagandist's cause as logically and/or morally correct — or when the contrary idea has grown powerful to the point that it must be addressed.

Many countries and organizations have controlled their internal information flow by establishing monopolies and/or strict controls over mass media and other internal media. China offers a current example. The People's Republic relies on both exclusion and a virtual state monopoly as an information source. The "news" is what the government officials of the centralized party apparatus say it is. Google, which many people in the West point to as an embodiment of informational freedom, operates only under restraints in the People's Republic. Email, chat rooms and blogging services are generally unavailable or liable to official shutdown. Searches on forbidden topics and organizations are blocked or lead to what BBC has called "condemnatory articles." YouTube, very popular in the West, is also essentially blocked, with near-zero traffic.

Why? It's obvious. Because otherwise the people of the People's Republic may actually start talking to one another in ways uncoordinated by the authorities. Private gripes and ideas of individuals may

---

29 An example from personal experience follows. In graduate school I attended a summer session on survey research methodology put on by the University of Michigan's famous Institute for Social Research. Michigan is known for such methodological expertise. A Harvard Ph.D. candidate in public health also attended. During a break she observed, "You know what we say at Hah-vard, that you folks at Michigan know *how* to ask the questions, but we at Hah-vard know *what* questions to ask." You may guess my response. I think this anecdote says more than enough about Harvard's relationship with the rest of the world.

align, inform publics and acquire social force. Autonomous social action may result, which is authority's worst nightmare because it renders authority superfluous. An effective prevention has been to pull the plug, which works as long as it can be enforced. The typical American, I notice, seems to have difficulty understanding how effective this has been, and does not seem to realize that the informational notions he carries in his head about China (and elsewhere) don't exist on the whole in China, where, as a Chinese student told me, the universities have walls around them. The information superhighway is closed.[30]

Sociologically speaking, mass media are important for national unification and for creating and maintaining cohesion in political parties, movements and interest groups. State-owned/controlled media have therefore been a norm in many parts of the world, e.g., many developing nations and Islamic nations, where authorities would never dream of letting something so important as the media of mass communication to be placed in hands other than their designees. Communication systems shape social reality. In authoritarian systems media prop up or extend the elite group's power. The same is true of organizations and their internal media, which tend, *ad nauseam*, to cheerlead and otherwise celebrate management and its quite often-vacuous initiatives.

An unauthorized (uncontrolled) channel of communication threatens an established order because it offers alternatives to official interpretation. Historically this has been called heresy. Of course virtually any elite or would-be elite is likely to complain of and attempt to hinder contrary information. It is a very natural impulse, e.g., even in America, which the naïve imagine as having enjoyed untrammeled freedom of press, during the Civil War, under President Lincoln the "great emancipator," a number of U.S. newspapers were suppressed and/or forced to be "loyal" to the Union cause. The naturalness of this censorious impulse explains why the First Amendment was thought necessary. Nowadays the American liberal democratic left complains

---

30 For examples, many current Chinese students I meet don't appear to know or care that that Mao Tse-Tung won a three-man contest with Hitler and Stalin for the title of greatest mass murderer of the Twentieth Century, or that American news media recently and effusively marked the 20th anniversary of something called, in America, the Tiananmen Square Massacre, but which in China is officially not recognized as anything. Interestingly, China's government treated recent ethnic unrest as a call for more effective cultural centralization, which means even more government information control is apparently in the works, while Americans tended to frame it as a civil rights issue. One billion people may as well live on a different planet with a different history and values.

about AM talk radio formats, which have been largely given over to conservative programming, and there is talk of resurrecting a "fairness doctrine" which would require stations carrying these views to provide airtime for liberal views. Conservatives in turn have complained about National Public Radio as a bastion of leftist ideology disguised as news, demanding that Congress cut off support, and they denounce the "mainstream" news media as ideologically biased to the left. All these are attempts to control either by exclusion or by mandating content or simply by shouting down opposition.

Bans, censorship boards, and restrictive licensing and registration for purposes of monitoring have often been used and attempted. Public relations firms and lobbyists are required to register with the U.S. State Department if they are acting as foreign agents, i.e., representing the interests of foreign clients in the U.S. by sowing foreign propagandas within the country, a common enough practice, but one which is regarded as dangerous enough that it requires registration. Or, quite commonly, organizations may have policies that prohibit employees from talking to outside media without management's prior approval, at threat of dismissal.

Loss of, or neglect of, the control of the flow of information allowed all sorts of political and religious heresies to spread, as when European political philosophers started publishing books back in the 1600s arguing that legitimate government was a "social contract" which the people could justly dissolve if rulers violated it. Kings and governments much preferred the idea of a "divine right of kings" to rule, a right and obligation bestowed by God, wherein obedience to authority was God's will and disobedience an affront to God as well as his earthly representative, the king. Hence from the first, kings licensed printing presses, banned books and pamphlets, as did the Church. The Church developed a control system whereby it gave its *imprimatur* (meaning "let it be printed") as a seal of approval to unobjectionable reading material and also published lists of books it had banned for corrupting the faith. Naturally, books on the "social contract" were banned, too. The Church finally gave up this practice only in relatively recent times, in 1966, some centuries after the informational horse had departed the barn. Book banning apparently was looking increasingly bad in an age dominated by the mass values of individualism and mass democracy. Also church officials apparently finally learned that merely adding a book to its *Index Librorum Prohibitorum* caused interest (and sales) to greatly increase, which illustrates yet another reason why it is often sensible for propagandists to ignore unwelcome ideas. Denouncement may help spread the dangerous ideas by providing free airtime. It also may create a psychological situation that might be called the "lure of the forbidden" that so fascinates some people. A sort of psychological syllogism is at work here: "the valuable is hidden, this is hidden, therefore it is valuable." [31]

To show how pragmatic propaganda can be, however, promoters and propagandists, long ago learned a valuable pecuniary lesson concerning the banned, censored and the hidden — controversy over condemned information-products can be used as a sales or recruiting tool. "*They* don't want you to see this" has proved a powerful attractant. Consider, for instance, how commercially beneficial the periodic controversies concerning hip-hop and rap music lyrics on themes of misogyny and cop killing have proved to the owners and promoters of these musical products. Such entertainment products are owned and distributed by mega-corporations, so it is absurd to think them revolutionary — although the genre may have been started out that way. Controversy promotes the product. Pop entertainer Janet Jackson's "accidental" breast exhibition on primetime Super Bowl television made much more of an impression than did the musical performance. Controversy, cold-bloodedly contrived or not, just provides more opportunities to augment the flow of information and also to sell products. May some organization ban this book!

So-called *Flak* sometimes proves useful to exclude or silence. Here unwelcome new information and its adherents are attacked viciously and shown as illogical, hateful, evil and otherwise repugnant. Attacks are often personal, directly or by implication. Op-eds, essays, book reviews, news articles, talking-head interviews, etc. may be used to deliver flak. The usefulness of this tactic varies and, like all others, it requires judgment in application, for it may excite some audiences

---

31 At about the age of 13, I somehow learned of Jack Kerouac's famous work on beat culture, *On The Road* (New York: Viking Press, 1957). Instead of being housed in general circulation, it was sequestered in the adult section of the local library. It was obviously too dangerous a book to leave on the shelves, which made it a very interesting book indeed. I obtained a copy and, looking back, was very much influenced by it because of this odor of the forbidden, this promise of arcane knowledge. A few years ago I tried to reread this book that I once thought so entrancing and found it dull beyond words. Although it seemed like fun at one time, I have slowly come to agree with Truman Capote's assessment of Kerouac's work — it's not writing, it's typing.

into paying more attention. But if the flak is based on values strongly held by the target audience the tactic may succeed in marginalizing the views in question and the people who hold them — e.g., denouncing as "racist" recent "tea party" demonstrations designed to protest taxation. Even though this criticism has little if any substance, it appears to have kept tea party topics out of the forum of serious national discussion. For even the mere accusation of racism in modern America is usually sufficient to either silence, drive from the field or morally taint any political foe, racism (which is often difficult to define) being in this era an absolute crime against elite sanctioned values that permeate mass education and entertainment systems. Who can even defend someone accused of racism?

An informational monopoly might be nice from the vantage point of the propagandist, but is not essential or practical, especially in these days of general literacy and near-universal media access where many channels and sources compete. Complete monopoly may not even be possible in politically open societies, or not worth the effort, so one must think in terms of the practical. A qualified monopoly or dominant presence in prestige media is sufficient. Setting up as a known source, an expert in some particular field, is one way of achieving this. Harvard, for example, is such a great place from which to promulgate ideas because it was among the first American universities. A Harvard presence lends radiance even to the dullest mediocrity, and is equivalent to occupying the informational high ground. Similarly, environmental news is dominated by the voices of a very small number of organizations that perpetually offer their expert services. Think tanks aim to achieve this as well.

Bureaucracy and Informational Control

Bureaucratic organization should be fundamentally regarded as a device to control the flow of information. Think of the pyramidal-shaped organizational chart that schematically represents the typical bureaucracy: formal reporting channels connect leaders, layers, departments and functionaries (individuals). Orders come down and reports pass up along them. As was laid down in the introduction, bureaucracy and propaganda came into the world together, much like conjoined twins. A bureaucracy provides the very situation that defines propaganda, where persons with access to an event can selectively release information about it in such a way as to benefit themselves.

Propaganda thus becomes an essential administrative function. Many administrators succeed almost entirely by controlling the flow of information, although this often described, euphemistically, as having good "skills" in "public relations" or "communication," although usually in my experience when someone says, "We are having a communication problem" this means I am not doing what they want. Administrators take credit for the work and ideas of their employees. Some hire only people whom they do not fear for being smarter, or more talented, ambitious or brazen than themselves. They isolate potential competitors. They selectively pass information uphill and downhill. Secrets are kept. Those best at this get promoted; they get "noticed." The best of the best may end up atop, or facilitating and enabling those at the top, while unadorned efficacy results only in more work. It is more important to take credit, to align, and to justify one's self than to do meaningful work. Put another way, the meaningful work performed in the modern bureaucracy is to take credit, align and justify. Creating new programs, sound and fury, and busy work for others is a good way to do this. The bywords of modern organizational communication are, "Take the credit and dodge the blame." [32]

The bureaucracy's formal informational channels are openly disregarded only at one's peril. To go outside of the "chain-of-command" and thus "back-door" some official or one's boss is a cardinal sin that may be rewarded by dismissal, marginalization, disciplinary action or the assignment of ignominious work. Another good way to get oneself fired or marginalized is to start sending memos throughout the organization that challenge the way things are being done. However, if such tactics work it may possibly lead to recognition "from above" and promotion. Informal networks of communication are also a good way to gain power in a bureaucracy — and often contain more truth and useful information than the official ones, which are clogged with the doubletalk language of *officialese*.

---

32   See Robert Jackal's work, *Moral Mazes* (New York: Oxford University Press, 1988). Also the already referred-to work of Altheide and Johnson, *Bureaucratic Propaganda*, which consists of case histories showing, among other things, how bombardment damage numbers were rigged in the Vietnam War, how social work services were numerically simulated, and even how evangelical crusaders rigged the appearance of mass participation. An eye-opening work!

A university may provide a good case study of effective information control, but the situation is much the same in any modern bureaucratic corporation The university president, the chief administrator, functions by controlling the flow of information in multiple directions — the board of trustees, to which the president reports, receives a highly selected arrangement of information at its regular meetings. Many personnel hours are spent in preparing this information so as to show the President and his minions in the best light possible. Good things are caused by the president's programs; bad things caused by sinister outside forces such as labor unions, the faculty and the economy.

Information is also carefully customized as it moves in other directions. Moving outward to the community, an office of university communications, staffed by about ten full time employees, releases information to local news media announcing new programs, paradigms, excellence, and transformative change. The cost of small raises for the faculty is blamed for budget shortfalls, but expenses in multi-million dollar increments to pet programs favored by the president are not mentioned, e.g., a "technology corridor," which to the naïve sounds like it leads somewhere definite, but no one knows exactly where or how, employs a number of remarkably well-paid administrators. Annual "state-of-the-union" style speeches by the president, delivered in parallel with press releases and simultaneous web-casting, announce yet more "transformational change" and the arrival of a "new learning paradigm" and "mass customization." The audience is packed with the many university administrators and their employees who report to them — it is important politically to be seen — who, massed together, simulate a fair-sized crowd. Vigorous and prolonged applause is general. Standing ovations common. A television news report unfavorable to the university administration becomes the subject of concerned telephone calls by university administrators and their communication personnel to the station's news and business managers, factual inaccuracies are claimed, and the report disappears from the station's story archives. The university begins advertising on that station's news program that same week.

Downwards in the university bureaucracy, newsletters and group emails resound with the triumphs of the administration. An unauthorized blog set up by some of the faculty is denounced as hurtful. In response, university administrators set up a dozen quasi-official blogs, using administrators (meaning that everything is ghostwritten by staff) and also recruiting students to write on the topic of the day, some of which are trite almost beyond belief, but which still take up space in the available channels. Rhetoric and administrative functions wax while faculty and departments silently wane — for departments have little control over the communication channels except to report up to them. Faculty governance meetings with administrators become time-wasting exercises in head-patting placation and extensive PowerPoint presentations designed to take up time that could have been spent answering questions. Truth and beauty reign. The President receives a 150 thousand dollar annual "longevity" bonus to stay three more years. Enrollments decrease, but that's the economy.

Communication Formats

Over-familiarity has perhaps led to an under-appreciation of the power of common communication formats. Here I am talking about simple (but tremendously effective) modes of packaging information that exist primarily to impose self-serving control on its flow. Among the most common are the deductive argument — where one lays down a thesis followed by its proofs, inverted pyramidal style as used in straight news journalism, the problem/solution format used in pro-posals and, finally, simple juxtaposition of images and sound as done in film editing.

Regarding the deductive argument, which applies some general principle to a specific instance, Aristotle pointed out that the only two essential parts of a persuasive presentation are a thesis statement and proof, an informational arrangement that has been well verified in twentieth-century experimental research. State your case and prove it, Aristotle advised, in that order. All else can be considered mere orna-ment. Distracting noise.

Does it work? Yes, definitely, in writing, court cases, debates, job interviews, term papers, reports, meetings, etc. It's easy to use — and audiences react favorably because it is so simple. It removes all ambi-guity; the audience does not need to guess or imply or work or con-clude anything because the source has done all this work for them. The assumption that an audience is cognitively lazy is usually a safe bet in propaganda. So the main point comes first, always. Instead of meandering narrative that arrives finally at a conclusion, all the while the listener wondering where this story is going, the communicator states the main point that he wants the listener to conclude at the very beginning, e.g., "Ladies and gentlemen of the jury, I am going to show you that the accused John Doe is guilty of the premeditated murder in the first degree of his wife, Jane Doe, because he planned the murder, lied to the police about his alibi, had her bloodstains in his car and on his person, in addition to taking out a million-dollar insurance policy the week before her violent death." And the rest of the trial becomes, in essence, a systematic delivery, a demonstration, of this set of proofs.[33]

Regarding what I just called the *deductive argument* style, I use this phrase because this type of persuasive presentation is ubiquitous and generally effective: lay down a thesis and prove it is so. Logically, the persuader merely delivers a syllogism. Virtually all presentations can be considered persuasive, by the way, because the presenter is trying to convince an audience that something is or is not the true way of things.

Moving on, inverted pyramidal style is the writing format used in news reporting; journalists and public relations professionals use it to give shape to their stories. It is so named because the reporter lays down a summary lead, which is the main idea compacted into a sentence or two, followed by the main points of the story in decreasing order of importance, becoming narrower and narrower. It was designed so editors could cut stories to fit the space available either in publication or broadcast, this space is known as the "Newshole" and is what remains after advertising space has been sold and apportioned, and despite the cuts still maintain story coherence. Inverted pyramidal style not only facilitates browsing, but also functions as a useful guide for quick, workman-like writing. Journalistic convention calls for balanced, fair reporting, so quotes from two sides will often be opposed, even if the story has multiple "sides." Journalism necessarily tends to simplify, which is especially desirable when using the format for propaganda purposes.

---

33 Regarding explicit versus implied conclusions, I generally advise students to do all the thinking for the intended audience, to make explicit all conclusions. In a word, never rely on a mass audience to reach a conclusion, because many people simply need to be led through the process and will not see the connection between the dots unless someone draws the line and underscores it. I call this "The 2 + 2 Rule of Communication," where 2 + 2 does not equal 4 unless the speaker or writer says explicitly that it does.

The "angle" or "framing" of stories is vital in inverted pyramidal style and can be easily done to achieve any number of differing slants, usually to accord with pre-existing clichés or stereotypes. For example, a story on welfare can be framed in various ways, almost at will, simply by crafting the appropriate lead and headline to tell either a story of welfare abuse, or bureaucratic inefficiencies in service delivery, or alleviating human misery, or government helping people overcome poverty and achieve their potential. In practice, the story content is selected to fit to the lead rather than the other way around. It is a style or recipe that lends itself to industrial hack writing, which is a dietary staple both in propaganda and journalism. That many prominent propagandists have risen up from the ranks of journalists attests to the indispensability of the news format in controlling the flow of information.[34]

Another common format of information control is the proposal. Proposals have fantastic potential power. They create something new by means of the power of language and are usually written in the problem-solution format. The idea in their composition is to entrain the audience into some logically inexorable progress of thought, which has all been laid down beforehand by the proposal's writer, where problem X is to be solved by the application of solution Y, which is of course the solution/product belonging to the proposal writer's organization. Proposals are the universal medium of organizational advancement.

Juxtaposition, as is universally done in film editing and novels, is also potentially powerful. By associating two or more concepts or images an author/editor can present a case that even an illiterate can connect. Films and mass entertainment can be so effective in propaganda because the thinking and emoting has been pre-prepared. Understanding becomes visceral without the difficulty of thoughtfulness. This well suits human nature. In film we merely see and hear. *The Eternal Jew*, a propaganda film made by the Nazis in 1940, juxtaposes murky oriental-sounding music to footage of praying Polish Jews used in the "documentary." An image of teeming cockroaches is sandwiched gratuitously within the segment. Simply put, explains the narrator, Jewish houses are dirty. This simple juxtaposition of four unrelated elements, a narration that holds it together, the music and

---

34 The fact that the "angle" is more important than the reality allegedly represented by the story is celebrated in an old journalistic maxim: *Never let the facts get in the way of a good story.*

sets of previously unrelated images, creates an appearance of a coherent reality. This is why propagandists love film and video. I should note here that I see no clear difference between the documentary and propaganda. They seem largely interchangeable terms. Film appears to be the greatest mass propaganda medium to date, although one mustn't entirely discount books and newspapers.[35] Online formats show great promise at exceeding even film's possibilities.

All these formats have achieved ubiquitous prominence because they can be used to build or represent self-serving realities using select truths, facts, data and information. Facts can be tendentiously chosen, with inconvenient facts and opinions ignored or dealt with via straw man methods. The formats themselves lend the appearance of concrete substance and authority to what otherwise would be just a random junk-pile of facts and factoids. The formats can be as deceptive to their writers as they are to their audiences. By marshaling information in these ways and putting it to work for a purpose, any response or resistance to it is accordingly made more difficult. The responder is virtually forced to respond in kind, e.g., the murder case example above would likely see John Doe hanged if his attorney could not present a professionally-assembled counter-case employing a full, well-elaborated set of counterproofs. The advantage gained in the application of these formats almost always accrues to the organizations and bureaucracies that employ professionals who are so steeped in these information control formats as to become second nature (which is one reason why so many John Does have been hanged).

Therefore, control the flow of information.

---

35 Fritz Hippler directed the documentary *The Eternal Jew,* produced in 1940 under the auspices of the Nazi leadership. It's a long film, and often tedious for today's more media–savvy audiences, as it is essentially a detailed liner argument of the sort that one would find developed in a book. Modern directors would go about this task much more quickly. But as far as illustrating principles of propaganda, it is wonderful. It was made for popular consumption among a people, the Germans, who, on the whole, were probably much more literate than mass audiences of today. It was a message from their government.

The Second Commandment

REFLECT THE VALUES AND
BELIEFS OF THE AUDIENCE

Propaganda works most effectively by piggybacking on beliefs and values that are already in people's heads, and not by trying to install entirely new cognitive equipment. It must therefore reflect or align with extant values and beliefs of its audience. The propagandist either directly evokes these values or threatens them with so-called fear appeals by "going negative." [36]

For example, when the Nazi's wanted to increase the level of anti-Semitism in the German public they did this by making the documentary film *The Eternal Jew*, which made a number of damning claims in the context of strongly held German cultural values: (1) Jews did not like to work and instead preferred to turn the intrinsically valued

---

36 The modern propagandist leaves the installation of new beliefs to the large, but slower-moving engines of socialization such as universal public education and mass entertainment. There are, of course, many beliefs and values that are culturally transmitted. Changing these is slow, long-term work, not that this is beyond the province of propaganda, but usually propagandists are more pragmatic and immediate in their outlook.

creative work and craftsmanship of "host peoples" into mere com-modities to be traded indiscriminately (2) Jews were unclean and dis-orderly, both civically and in the home, thriving on the sicknesses and sores of other people which they inflamed in order to exploit them, and (3) a visceral kicker reserved for the end of the film, they lacked the innate German love and respect for animals, and instead killed cattle cruelly by the method of kosher slaughter. The documentary graphi-cally detailed the latter with close ups of the dying cattle — spurting arteries, last bovine gasps and all. I have had students leave the class-room at this part of the film because this scene was too much for them. But by such techniques the film tried to clearly establish that the Jews were the spiritual and psychological opposites of the Germans. The film also established, for its intended audience, the socially progressive nature of the Nazi program of scientific government by heroic authori-ties who were not afraid to confront the eternal enemies of mankind. Progress is a central Western value.

Nowhere in *The Eternal Jew* is it suggested or stated that Jews should be killed, deported or concentrated into camps.[37] This would be ugly business. Instead the film continually hammers upon a major value triad common to the audience: the intrinsic value of creative work, orderliness and compassion for animals. If the film had urged that Jews be killed, it would have violated a basic value of the audience, for one can't just go around advocating the killing of a whole people. Instead the Jews were framed as a worldwide, historical social problem and the film left it at that. This case was demonstrated on the basis of all sorts of information, comparative evidence, partial truths and quotes from authoritative sources, all juxtaposed in an overwhelm-ingly long and detailed narrative that almost induces coma in a mod-ern audience. But it is a film designed for a literate public, a longish lin-ear argument almost constructed like reading from a book, which was totally appropriate for pre-television age citizens with a long average attention span as compared to today's mass audiences that are accus-tomed to flickering from one dazzling instant to the next. They had been preconditioned by a public education system that had steeped

---

37 The concentration camp appears to have been a British invention before the turn of the twentieth century and was used to contain Afrikaners, who were Dutch farmers who resisted British colonialism, during the Boer War in South Africa. However, it was also used about the same time in Cuba by the Spanish colonial government to contain rebels and insurrectionists on the eve of the Spanish-American War, many of whom died in captivity.

them in some level of common shared culture and beliefs about the world, a people who looked to authority, government and education for answers. There is no ranting, no raving in the film. It is much like a public health documentary in tone. It unwinds in the expected voice of the documentary genre, objective, even quasi-scientific, except perhaps for a few slips into discussion of the "idealism of our young people" as compared to the egoistical, cunning attributed to young Jews. And of course the film also drew upon ideas, beliefs or folk knowledge that many people already held about the Jews — information that was culturally available if not unavoidable in entertainment, folklore and everyday conversation — that the Jews were wanderers, outsiders, urban (a people without farmers, without workers, observes the narrator) who subsisted through a base sort of commerce. A student asked me how the intended audience could have believed it. The response to that question is *why wouldn't they have believed it?* For in large part the film consisted of things the intended audience already knew or felt to be true — it just systematized this information, concentrated it and applied it to interpreting the meaning/function of the Jews in the construction of the Nazi worldview.

Similarly, a few years previous, *The Triumph of the Will*, a documentary by the famous cinematographer Leni Riefenstahl, had celebrated Nazism with a parallel set of utterly wholesome values. While *The Eternal Jew* dealt darkly with a social problem, *Triumph of the Will* was all light and glory. The new Nazi government was already delivering the goods that the German people deserved: hope, a future for the children, economic and social progress, constructively employed people in public works programs, *Wurst* for breakfast, and thriving communities where the worker was valued for meaningfully contributing to the social order. Nazism was the vehicle for a German Renaissance, a sort of "change one could believe in" suitable for that time and place, and a radical reversal of economic and political woes suffered by Germany in the immediately preceding years. The film affirms the values of optimism, clean living, work, community and social order, and uses as a focal point the annual Nazi party rally in Nuremberg, of course associating all these good things with the advent of Hitler and the Nazis. One cannot sell a modern mass political movement based on death and destruction. The Jews accordingly do not figure at all into Riefenstahl's vision, which is juxtaposed and edited from thousands of hours of raw footage into a value-collage, and delivered without narration. There is no need for narration. The images and music tell the story right from when the savior-archetype figure of Hitler descends from the heavenly clouds in his airplane as the film begins. This image conveys a messianic meaning that an illiterate could absorb, perhaps without even being aware of doing so. Students are often astonished by the wholesomeness of *Triumph of the Will* because they have been reared on the stereotyped images of Nazism that fill current American entertainment, i.e., the Holocaust. But while the Jews and others provided a convenient threat to mobilize against, and were treated as the embodied attack on Germanic values, such was certainly not what generally appealed to the masses regarding Nazism. Instead the citizen-viewer would have seen clean-limbed young men frolicking in an orderly campground, a huge outdoor event on a field with hundreds and hundreds of perfectly arrayed tents laid out with the precision expected of a model city. The youths join together joyfully to help prepare their communal breakfast in an outdoor kitchen. There is food and music for everybody.[38] On motorcade routes and elsewhere, women smile and wave, holding their children up to see and be seen by the Führer. Crowds of thousands of happy, genuinely excited people line the streets as the motorcade passes, with Hitler standing in an open car, unprotected before the crowds, a feat that no recent U.S. president appears to be able to do in safety. There is virtually no military presence. Just a few uniforms functioning as an honor guard and to contain the crowds. Instead disciplined wholesome young men assemble in formation with shovels, symbolic of the work force of the nation. It is no wonder that some Americans, a notable example being industrialist Henry Ford, admired the Nazi movement and its apparently wholesome effects on both youth and the economy. Ford thought that America could do with some of that same medicine.

Long, long before, Aristotle had instructed political persuaders to keep in mind the basic elements of happiness — i.e., the things that people valued. Political or commercial propaganda that does not ultimately aim somehow at happiness is doomed to irrelevance. Aristotle

---

38 I once heard a quote attributed to Hitler that I have never been able to verify. If it is not something he actually said, however, then it is something that he could as well have said, considering his preferred methods in conducting mass demonstrations: "Give me a brass band and I will lead the German people to Hell." Recordings of SS marching songs that I have heard sound much like polkas to me, despite their sometimes bloody lyrics, a popular musical form, and another example of propaganda reflecting the values/tastes of the audience.

listed elements of happiness as, among other things, the secure and independent enjoyment of goods, health, wealth, friendship, good children, good birth (meaning being native born and not being of the desperate lower classes) and a pleasant old age.[39] These are essentially the same sort of psychological erogenous zones that American politicians (or more precisely, their speechwriters, communication teams, pollsters and party machinery) still attempt to access and stimulate in voters.[40]

Despite their apparent polarization, the chief political parties in America merely differ somewhat in how they appeal to different sets or permutations of values and beliefs, as various people may hold many of the same values and beliefs, but nevertheless rank them quite differently in regard to relative importance. Republicans of course call out for more individualism and less government, personal freedom as guaranteed by the absence of government constraint, "traditional values" such as religion and personal responsibility and a work ethic that equates with the ability to be independent and seek to create one's own wealth and, therefore, happiness. Democrats call more to communitarianism, belief in scientific public administration, personal opportunity as guaranteed by government and overarching social responsibility delivered via public apparatus; happiness is distributed equitably, in theory, by the state. The parties are probably more alike than they are different, and the disagreements are often over means rather than end-values.

Some values and beliefs that must be simultaneously appealed to are paradoxical in their nature — e.g., Americans value good, old-fashioned hard work by the individual as a way of "moving up" socially (and developing something called "character" which is thought important by many people). At the same time Americans see the value of altruistic social programs to help the unemployed or the less fortunate to rise, or at least not to plummet, i.e., the so called social safety net.[41]

---

39 See Book I of *Rhetoric*, in which Aristotle discusses a cluster of values and topics that inform political rhetoric of his time and that still undergird the political propaganda of our time.

40 Aristotle also predicted that mass democracy turned inevitably to tyrannical demagoguerywhen unscrupulous leaders secured the votes of the unsophisticated and uneducated masses by means of blandishments, e.g., the promise of eternal free lunches.

41 Professor John Tropman of the University of Michigan has written a useful book on this topic in which he suggests the existence of an American social ethic that is suspended, in effect, in a state of dynamic tension between opposed but equally cherished values. This is a very Aristotelian way to look at ethics — as the mean between harsh, undesirable extremes. See *The Catholic Ethic in American Society* (San Francisco: Jossey Bass 1995).

Such values can be thought of as the anchoring points of a continuum of sorts, where an individual may have a balance point somewhere in between the oppositional extremes at each end. The individual's preferred balance point may determine whether he is called a liberal or a conservative, but virtually no one utterly rejects either value, they merely lean more toward one than the other. The political parties strike a somewhat different balance between these sorts of value extremes, e.g. government regulation versus personal freedom, or income redistribution with public services through taxation as opposed to minimal taxation policies under free market economics. In these matters the parties strategically appeal to different clusters of variously weighted beliefs held by constituencies, whose tastes are usually determined more by their social-economic circumstances rather than some sort of rational evaluation of Truth and the Good. Rationalism more often follows circumstances than it precedes them.[42] Therefore, different things seem reasonable to people who exist under different circumstances, e.g., those who aren't paying for it see the worth of income redistribution, while the individual who has an interest in maintaining the status quo sees many reasons why things must be arranged just they way they are. The question of audience values is always a foremost consideration in propaganda.

Audience beliefs equate with so-called common knowledge, too. These are the things that virtually everyone knows or refers to; they are of course culturally conditioned. They change but slowly; old ones may drop off while new ones intrude. So-called *stereotypes* are such beliefs. The American cowboy, the urban drug dealer, the pimp, the businessman, the Arab sheik, the farmer, the southerner, the French waiter, the noble savage, the Irish cop, the lumberjack, the good-hearted whore, the republican businessman, the momma's boy, the liberal professor — you probably have stock pictures in your head of all these and many more. There are also stories, urban legends, phrases

---

42 A whole stream of behavioral persuasion research beginning in the 1950s supports this contention. When people commit publicly to some course of behavior, even in a minor way, they later construct rational defenses of it. The Chinese attempted this trick in so-called brainwashing of American POWs in the Korean War. They would have POWs write and publicly read an essay mildly critical of social conditions in the U.S., in exchange for better treatment of the prisoners. Some attitude change had to inevitably follow the public confession, however trite. See Edgar Schein's "A Study of Attempted 'Brainwashing'" in *Readings in Social Psychology*, third edition (New York: Holt, Rinehart and Winston, 1958).

that circulate, and many pervasive idioms in speech. To speak in other terms is simply to baffle. Plus, it is not very efficient from a cognitive processing point of view — the person who has to stop and think about meanings is spending too much energy and paying too much attention therefore to be easily propagandized. It is far easier to traffic in commonplaces, in the things already imagined as known. Hence, the existence of what I call the *propaganda of mediocrity*, where politicians and corporate leaders communicate in dreadfully stock phrases. They do this because steering down the middle of the river of cognition is often the safest, easiest and most effective course. Mediocrity may be a protective screen.

Phrases and allusions that were common knowledge of the nineteenth century and the first half of the twentieth simply confuse modern audiences, however. For example, one cannot compare today's politician to Prometheus, instead one shows how he worked his way up from humble origins, that standard old potboiler, or overcame adversity, or dedicated himself to community service among the disadvantaged, and even more of these dreadful stock phrases. If one speaks of "Plato" today, much of the audience may be hearing instead, "Play Doh," that brightly colored aromatic modeling clay sold as a child's toy.

Continuing with typical stock ideas and beliefs, virtually everybody in America thinks of themselves as middle class, a hopelessly flawed notion because most people everywhere are lower class by virtue of working by absolute necessity for a wage/salary.[43] Politicians, however, must always refer to the "American middle class" to cater to this popular delusion, or risk grating upon the sensibilities (or insensibilities) of their audience. Saving the middle class was, accordingly, a major theme in the 2012 elections. Many Americans would be upset that someone, even themselves, might regard them as lower class, for this status connotes undesirable moral as well as economic qualities. Moreover many of these "middle class" people believe unthinkingly in a materialistic consumeristic sort of progress, making them highly susceptible to beguiling new programs with messianic overtones (which, being fundamentally propagandistic in nature, are usually just recycled old ideas and values) that advance promises in the form of vague, liturgical incantations based on science, technology, medicine,

---

43 See my "Misperceptions of Middleclasshood," (in press) a paper based on extensive focus group findings and which explores the vital meanings that a belief in *middleclasshood* holds for those who subscribe to it.

education as a miraculous social leveler, the American dream. Easy loans for home ownership, renewable energy, fuel-producing algae that will "free us of foreign oil" and "saving the environment" will in turn rescue us all.

The propagandist cannot disappoint in the matter of delivering commonplaces, at risk of losing resonance with the known, familiar world of the audience. If one really listens, consciously and deliberately, to the modern political speech one will likely find it filled with dreadfully trite language and tired idioms.[44] A very effective prophylaxis against propaganda, by the way, is simply to pay keen mental attention to the meaning of what is being said and not said, being "heedful," in the old sense of this word, of thoughtful absorption.[45] For example, by asking yourself what a speaker means by "transformative change" or "reengineering the organization" you will likely soon see that the speaker has no more idea than you do — anything close to a definite meaning that such phrases may acquire is achieved through the projection of the audience members' inner values onto this rhetorical fog. The listener is anxious about the way things are going — and therefore imagines seeing what is on his mind, i.e., "change" rather than mere nebulous language. Suggestibility wins. A professional corporate speechwriter once told me that her art consisted in writing a speech that sounded very firm and authoritative but really said very little in the way of specifics. The listeners would fill in the blanks via projection.

Surveys and Metrics

The reason that modern politicians and marketers, who are much the same in their methods, spend so much effort and money on polls and focus groups is to find out as exactly as possible what people are

---

44 George Orwell wrote a wonderful essay that anyone who values their own intelligence should read called "Politics and the English Language." It can be found online. Orwell makes the case that plain Anglo-Saxon-rooted English speaks Truth better than inflated Latin- and Greek-rooted words, and that leaders use this borrowed high-blown language for puffery and evasion.

45 Karl Weick calls attention to this use of the word "heedful" in his work on unsuccessful group interactions in his Mann Gulch article about a group of smoke jumpers who burned up in a Montana forest fire. See "The Collapse of Sensemaking in Organizations: The Mann Gulch Disaster" (*Administrative Science Quarterly*, Vol. 38, pp. 628-652, 1993).

currently carrying around in their heads, as well as demographic particulars, and how they are reacting to current events and issues, so that suitable appeals can be mass produced to fit them. Oxymoronically, this paradox is called "mass customization."

Reliable mass survey research techniques, also known as public opinion research or polling, only became possible in relatively recent times with the invention of statistical techniques to assess the accuracy (e.g., *margin of error* or *confidence intervals*) of relatively small random samples drawn from a much larger population.[46] These advances made it possible to efficiently sample from mass populations and then confidently infer characteristics (parameters) of the larger population based on those of the sample. All this technical knowledge arrived in the post World War II era. Since that time survey research has become an American institution. Such data lend themselves remarkably well to easy quantification and application in modern mass society, thus providing propagandists a way to safely navigate through the currents of public opinion. The U.S. government itself funds huge, very expensive, surveys that take place on an annual basis — e.g., the General Social Survey headquartered out of the National Opinion Research Center in Chicago. Another is the U.S. Census, which is becoming more intrusive each passing decade, and seemingly reaching beyond its constitutional purpose of allowing fair determinations to be made in political representation in the Congress.[47] Much survey data is public and stored in archives for use by social engineers of various sorts. Many other polls and surveys are proprietary, e.g., political parties, interest groups and commercial corporations routinely survey to better ride the seas of public opinion.

Focus groups offer another effective way of deeply probing values, vulnerabilities, gullibilities and beliefs of target populations. A focus group consists of, roughly, 6-15 persons chosen to represent a target audience, who are led through a series of questions and discussions by a "facilitator" for the purpose of probing opinions and reactions

---

46 Much of the statistical mathematics that made this possible came from agricultural science, where scientists were attempting to compare the characteristics of plant plots. Another famous statistical test, the "T-test," was invented by the Guinness Brewery personnel for quality control purposes.

47 Technically, a census includes all of a population, while a sample as used in a typical survey includes only a relatively small portion that is then used to infer the properties of the overall "population," as social scientists call it. Obviously a sample must reasonably well represent the population to be useful.

to ideas or products. A typical focus group might last an hour to 90 minutes, usually progressing from general to more specific questions and topics, and might be considered to act as a sort of cloud chamber as used by physicists to better see and understand the behaviors of atomic particles. In this case we are plotting human particles and their attitudes and behaviors relating to the formation of public opinion. The focus group provides a window on human actions and reactions in a simulated public opinion setting, as in real life people are parts of groups and communities, for public opinion is not generated in isolation but in social contexts. Within the focus group people collide, veer away, posture to themselves and others and grapple, and the results may cautiously be viewed as a reasonable approximation of the values and reactions of the larger mass public.

Conducting focus groups is a scientifically informed art, and although one must beware their results sometimes; if properly conducted they provide valuable data on audience likes and dislikes. They are routinely used to test and design products, advertisements, speech rhetoric (e.g., State of the Union speeches), and so forth. They are also used to help test and design mass surveys that can then be broadly applied on a more "industrial" mass scale than focus groups. Focus groups are also used to design alternate plots and endings of commercial films and entertainment — the endings and plot twists that the test-groups like the most are those used in the final edit. One might even design modern popular musical entertainment groups, picking this personality and that one, so as to best appeal to the eleven-year-olds that constitute a major segment of this market.

This gauging of values and reactions can become a very cold-blooded business. For example, back in the years of the Clinton presidency the First Family vacationed in the Western United States because democratic pollsters found in focus groups that many voters valued Western vacations as recreation. I suspect presidents, or, more accurately, their handlers, select (and publicize) the First Family's dogs and cats on the basis of focus group results; the Germans have not been the only nation with a sentimental love for animals. Consider though, that in some countries and cultures the notion of having a dog, an unclean animal, inside the house would incite only disgust; while an unclean animal in the house of a ruler of a nation might be seen as even more disgusting. Propagandists may employ such value-displays to inform "news" stories intended for widely different purposes and audiences.

Once again, it is by far easier for propagandists to work with the ideas preexisting in people's heads. Dislodging preexisting ideas by means of propaganda is often much more difficult than an original installation. Totalitarian dictators have exterminated whole classes of people for this reason, e.g., Stalin and Mao's mass killings of persons whom they thought likely to hold ideas inconvenient to the revolutionary sorts of monism demanded by official party worldviews. In corporate environments the old guard are merely fired (or forced into early retirement) and replaced with fresh new people unspoiled by annoying preconceptions about how the world should work.

The effective propagandist knows his audience well, often through direct experience and/or by keeping in constant touch with popular culture. Hitler, who saw propaganda as aimed at the masses for the purpose of gaining supporters, advised that propagandists should come from the masses, and not from elites who exist too far above the masses to truly understand them. Academics are often terrible propagandists, even when trying to act on their own behalf, because they are so self-absorbed or lost in their disciplines — it makes little difference which — that they are unaware of the values of their audience. As a result, they preach down to their audiences, annoy them, or talk above them and require too much cognitive effort on the part of audiences, and thus are simply incomprehensible. Members of social elites, especially ones subjected to intense peer group pressure or hubris, also are prone to this mistake. They are so committed to their own values/ideas that their propaganda takes on a prescriptive tone that has no appeal to a target audience that may not see itself in need of the treatment that is being prescribed.

Propaganda that does not somehow reflect core values and prior beliefs of the audience lacks both relevance and comprehensibility.

The Third Commandment

DISAMBIGUATE

A mbiguity is the enemy of propaganda.
Propaganda does not work well when there seem to exist only many shades of grey, so often the case in daily life. Instead, clear demarcations between starkly contrasted alternatives need be established, amplified or imagined, demarcations that mirror the propagandist's preferred interpretation of reality. These contrasts may be made between ideas, opinions, people, behaviors, products, organizations, or whatever. Even if no genuinely opposing ideas or alternatives exist, a perception of them can be suggested, and made discernable through the fog of events by simple, often arbitrary acts of interpretation, e.g., "There's us, the best, then there's all the rest."

Such dichotomies trap the cognitively unwary. Good/evil, black/white, liberal/conservative, urban/rural: persons who thoughtlessly stumble into such conceptualizations often may never be able to climb back out. Dichotomies can be natural or created, significant or insignificant, or merely an amplified nuance. I know an ambitious man who decided to commence a political career by running for county commissioner. He impressively won his race, upsetting a long-term and seemingly well-ensconced incumbent, by a strategy of creating and then amplifying an imaginary divide between what he had begun to call "West County" and "East County." West County, he contended, had always been slighted by East County. As a native West County son he would see this injustice corrected by making sure that West County received, at last, its fair share of road and park improvements and other services. He also ran a vigorously pro-gun campaign, to distinguish himself from the other candidate who was not talking about this issue at all, as no gun control matters had ever been taken up by the county commission, nor was there any intent to do so. Nevertheless, in addition to his East County/West County manifesto, he distributed pamphlets printed in hunter's orange that pictured himself with guns and in hunting situations, both as a child and an adult, declaring his absolute commitment to the Second Amendment: "It's your right!" This appealed not only to deeply held values of the many farmers and sportsmen of the county (following the Second Commandment) but also created an appearance of perceptual clarity on an issue that had really been no issue at all within the county until he made it one.

Disambiguation is achieved in a number of common ways: through acts of pure interpretation which might include expert, revelatory and/or authoritarian pronouncements on the meaning and nature of reality; through definitions and the naming or renaming of phenomena; through agitation propaganda which inflames or further polarizes preexisting class or social differences for the purpose of social mobilization or political action; through what I term *cartoon history*, worldviews and cosmologies which simplify perceptions of reality in ways that support the social goals of propagandists; and through the use of stories, folklore, myths, examples, parables, stereotypes and anecdotes that provide vivid paradigms of propagandistically desirable ideals or counter-ideals. In all cases, the propagandist attempts to make a complex, baffling and generally overwhelming objective reality more cognitively and subjectively manageable in ways that facilitate his or her goals.

Like highly processed fast food, which is specifically prepared to best facilitate ease of consumption, the propagandist cuts, dices, artificially colors, flavor enhances, packages and even predigests so as to make consumption as instant, interesting, painless and momentarily satisfying as possible. Neither product is made with true nutrition or quality of life in mind; although both must pass casual muster and take advantage of the infantile human need for immediate gratification, be it comfort derived from food, or to quell fears of the unknown, or to avoid boring, unpleasant or complicated matters that demand perhaps too much spiritual energy with which to wrestle. The propagandist fights your spiritual and psychological battles for you by proxy, as it were, providing his terms are accepted. In another sense, propaganda makes things dramatically simple in a cheapened way. One could say that propaganda functions as spiritual junk food. The audience consumes it because it is easier than the sort of nutritious eating that requires more planning and work.

The Interpretation of Meaning

Possibly the most important human right beyond life itself is that of the interpretation of the meaning and nature of reality, i.e., the old questions of why are you here and where you are going. It is also the right that people seem to give away most thoughtlessly, possibly because trying to exercise it can be so anxiety-producing. This is, in part, the "fear of freedom" in which psychoanalysts such as Erich Fromm trafficked.[48] The exercise of this right is also, in quite large part, "the pursuit of happiness" discussed by the philosopher-revolutionaries of the early American Republic.

But Everyman as his own priest and philosopher (two traditional interpretive callings) requires a degree of social and personal responsibility perhaps beyond the reach of most of the people much of the time. Some people also appear largely untroubled by thought. Power and prestige have accrued historically to those who have been able to succeed at this business of interpretation in ways that seem to satisfy. Usually these are higher order, absolute interpretations to the eternal questions, but delivered in such a way as to appeal to the need for instant gratification. "Change we can believe in" or "the stimulus package" sounds pretty good to someone who has just discovered his economic diaper is soiled. Such hard and fast interpretation is the very stuff of demagogic propaganda. Professional interpreters, hired for cash or fief arrangements, industriously formulate such versions of reality for their patrons.

---

48 Fromm's *The Fear of Freedom* (London: Kegan Paul, Trench and Trubner, 1942).

Interpreters also impose higher order meaning on the perceptually inchoate or emotionally unacceptable, e.g., "Your baby is with Jesus now in Heaven;" or "The layoff was caused by the economic downturn;" or the once-popular assimilation propaganda, "America is a melting pot;" or today's identity-politics slogan, "cultural diversity." Shamans, priestly classes, political elites have always specialized at this much-in-demand art. There are also modern political entrepreneurs who traffic in explanations, e.g., various think tanks and non-profit organizations do much the same today.[49] Simplified explanations and some notion of a higher order infuse daily existence with a degree of tranquility. Lack thereof creates severe anxiety, alienation or a deadly ennui. The propagandist opportunistically fills a market demand for these off-the-rack explanations, such that, as Jacques Ellul so memorably put it, "Everything is explained thanks to propaganda."

Indeed, everything is indeed explained thusly. Ideologies amount to prefabricated, standardized explanations of the world. Democrats, Republicans, Greens, Christian Fundamentalists, Conservatives, Liberals (modern ones, not the eighteenth century variety), Humanists, Marxists, Nazis, etc., all have two fundamental commonalities. First, they leave no loose hermeneutical ends; each understands the world, all of it — at least all of it that matters — each in its own way. Second, the explanations benefit their chief proponents who stand in a managerial or superior relationship to the world as it is thus explained. You can verify my two claims merely by listening.

There is also the necessary matter of social lubrication as provided by propaganda in regard to the hard, apparently unavoidable aspects of life. This is why Marx labeled religion as the opiate of the masses and Nietzsche dismissed Christianity as a slave religion, meaning that it consoles and placates the disadvantaged. When used for disambiguation, such doctrines help people accept an unfair lot in life and have seen extensive secular use in those many places where the rewards of hard work have been only more hard work. While much traditional social control ideology derives from religion, Marxism itself, with its credo of progressive historical class conflict and materialism, can be seen as just another disambiguating belief system that has benefited elite groups in the name of social justice. In this regard, Marxism

---

49 I do not suggest that all think tanks and non-profit organizations fit these criteria.

functions as just another slave religion.[50] While ostensibly oppositional, free-market economic theory can be used in the much same way — to ensure that much unpleasant work gets done by employees who have no realistic hope of ascending the class structure, the old elbow-grease-will-set-you-free myth. Scientism, the naively superstitious belief that science saves, also sees much service in administrative tale spinning. Administrators also routinely draw on physical and social scientists not only to inform, but to legitimate policies. Such diverging, often oppositional applications suggest that propaganda may be the most flexible of the arts. Regarding disambiguating beliefs, not everything is propaganda, but just about everything may be used for propagandistic purposes.

An example of this astonishing degree of flexibility is that explanations derived from Christianity have been used both to support and undermine oppressive social orders. The American civil rights movement was infused with the Old Testament story of the Exodus, which clarified and disambiguated a complicated era, setting the psychological stage for a large scale social movement, e.g., "Lord, set my people free and lead them to the Promised Land." Working in the opposite direction, religious stories facilitated bondage, as when higher order scriptural and sociological style interpretations provided justifications for slavery in nineteenth-century America. Slaves were identified as the progeny of Noah's son Ham and therefore had been biblically cursed as "hewers of wood and drawers of water."[51] Natural law type arguments, used as another type of high order disambiguation, have supported emancipation and women's suffrage, or the other way around — by arguing either that nature had made all free or had destined some people as slaves or "weaker vessels." The history of propaganda says that you can indeed have it both ways. Only with propaganda, can one have the cake, eat it and then redistribute it like the scriptural loaves and fishes, as can be seen by current American political trends. Propaganda is miraculous.

---

50 A couple of generations ago Schumpeter talked about Karl Marx the prophet. He also referred to Marxism as one of the great modern religions. Schumpeter is none too popular these days. See his *Capitalism, Socialism and Democracy* (London: Allen & Unwin, 1976). It was originally published in 1942.

51 A sociologically-styled justification of slavery can be found in Fitzhugh, who might be described as a American, southern version of Karl Marx, in his justifiably obscure book *Cannibals All*.

Propagandists routinely evoke absolutes to endorse merely convenient interpretations, infusing them with auras of factuality, inexo-
rability, necessity and legitimacy. For how can anyone hope to reasonably oppose God, Science, the Natural Order or the unfolding of
History? Equipping oneself even to attempt this kind of undertaking
requires uncommon character, knowledge, resources, perseverance
and generally some sort of organizational backing. Disambiguating
techniques are especially effective when paired with control of the flow
of information, in accord with the First Commandment, for a vivid
tale dominates in lieu of the alternative tale that would be provided
by an organized opposition. Moreover, because the thoughtless and
the harried tend not to systematically seek other explanations, sheer
human inertia abets propaganda.

It's really very simple, so simple that it often slips by unnoticed. "The
universe is arranged in just such a way," says the Official Interpreter of
Meaning, "Therefore, we must behave accordingly." Although I must
point out here that when the propagandist says "we" he usually really
means "you." Almost invariably The Way gives unto Caesar what is
Caesar's, and unto God what is God's, but both so often seem to be
working out of the same address.[52] Of course believers and insiders
(often the same people) don't generally see things quite this nakedly,
a view which they tend to dismiss as "cynical" or as griping of "the
disgruntled." The way, however, tends also to be maximally convenient
for these insiders.[53] Recollect, too, that propaganda technique is pragmatic to the point of almost infinite variability within circumstantial
parameters, so the same people who cry for "centralization" this year
will be advocating "local control" next year if a changing context
seems to require it. Beliefs may change or rotate, i.e., the content of the
propaganda, but the practice and techniques of propaganda remain
fairly constant.

---

52 Years ago an old man told me of a defining moment in his life that he experienced
back in his youth in Italy. He realized one day that the local nobility's estate and the
church shared the same hilltop. He had an epiphany of sorts, namely that the church
fathers and the upper classes shared the same interests in maintaining an obedient
lower working class.

53 Remember the tale of the emperor's new clothes. Today's emperor is surrounded by
propagandists who extol his wardrobe; and since the emperor is known to the people
only via second and third hand media accounts, the wardrobe comes to seem very
tangible indeed.

Using again the example of the Roman Catholic Church, another reason why the Church throve as a secular institution is because of its longstanding, functional monopoly on the interpretation of the meaning of reality. Its bureaucracy, self-identified as the One and True Church, delivered the only approved version of reality. Competing stories were explained away by being designated as heretical, dismissed as primitive folk beliefs or often were simply appropriated and recycled through the practice known as syncretism — e.g., many of the saints in the older hagiographies were ancient pagan deities who were appropriated because of their popular appeal.[54] It made little difference whether they were saints or ancient demigods, providing they kept the people on their knees instead of on their feet. Obdurate heretics could be burned alive, which was interpreted as being for the good of all concerned. Interpretive monopoly, it must be noted, was not an arrangement that the Church gave up willingly. It was wrenched away. Elites by their nature do not surrender such rights.[55]

Modern corporate organizational heretics may find themselves fired in a somewhat different way, whether for apostasy, or for merely not evincing sufficient reverence, or merely for the crime of not subscribing to the ideas of the inner circle. This too is interpreted away as contributing toward the greater good by corporate human resources professionals, who employ canned story lines that point out how firing is really best for the person being fired, because it lets them move on to "other opportunities" where presumably a form of happiness awaits that is derived from something corporate parlance calls "fit." Of course, such a story disambiguates at the expense of accuracy — but accuracy is often inconvenient, in addition to being overly complicated for the telling. Accuracy merely puts the average person to sleep. Also, generally, corporate elites use such stories to rationalize action already taken or decided — universal law, logic itself, then weighs in on the side of

---

54 Mysteries incomprehensible were consigned to God and became official "sacred" mysteries. "Faith" was circularly defined as being achieved by a belief in things that made no sense, thereby proving Faith.

55 Kings and Queens descended from Gods; thus the "nobility" were the best sort of people, and traditionally have been linked to universal order and the laying down of the social basics — e.g., the Divine Right of Kings to rule, codes of law, the so-called King's English (consider the King James Bible and its effects on standardization of belief and language), even on physical measures of reality such as the King's foot becoming the linear "foot."

the elites as they tell the story. This game, however played, is always designed for the house to win.

Still, in more modern times, it has been quite possible to get one-self killed by disagreeing (or simple by refusing to align) with an official disambiguation. Millions did in the "modern" twentieth century, e.g., Hitler's, Stalin's and Mao's victims. We should probably not try to explain away their crimes by attributing them to extraordinary social monsters — had it not been one of them some other death angel would have arisen amongst these interpretive cults.[56] Propaganda kills. Once installed, an officially promulgated interpretation will generally brook no rivals, or even audible grumbling, at least not on its own turf.[57] But the "true believer," or the convincing simulator of belief, is highly employable.[58]

In modern times, the leader who can express what corporate jargon calls "vision" is essentially an interpreter of meaning. The corporate vision functions as a disambiguating social cartography that sloganizes a world perceived as a set of goals, opportunities, perils, routes and destinations.[59] It imposes a manageable sense of order or

---

56 In no sense am I suggesting that these murderers were themselves victims of circumstances, but that we probably best understand them as the representative leaders of absolute schools of interpretation rather than as social anomalies. A good example of Stalin's attitude toward the problem of nonalignment with the official faith, or even suspected nonalignment, is the quote attributed to him, "No man, no problem." As Stanley Milgram so convincingly demonstrated, the average person is fifty percent likely to become a monster very quickly under the right set of conditions.

57 Apparent exceptions exist. Jacques Elull reports that even the party apparatus of the Soviet Union practiced a conspicuously virtuous form of self-criticism. The same is true of Maoist revolutionaries — but this is a special kind of criticism more like the confessional than the dialectic of true back-and-forth conversation. It is a performance designed to increase the credibility of the propagandists who appear more earnest and honest thereby. The reward of unauthorized social criticism, or simple disagreement, as the Marxists seemed to have no conceptualization of "loyal dissent," was exile or death.

58 See Eric Hoffer's sometimes astonishing book, *The True Believer: Thoughts on the Nature of Mass Movements* (New York: Harper & Row, 1951). Hoffer was a long-shoreman who wrote books, damned thoughtful ones. He believed that true believers were on the whole persons who, having failed at some important business of life, seized upon some ideology in compensation.

59 Of course, there exist other forms of social cartography that are more or less cultural in nature. See my paper discussing the social-cartographic functions of improvised Viking poetry and Rap/Hip Hop music. "Vikings as Rappers: The Icelandic Sagas. Hip Hop Across 8 Mile," in *Journal of Popular Culture* (42)(2). The basic idea is that people use stories and poetry to map out their social environment so that they can navigate and conquer it.

focus — *manageable* being the key word for corporate elites. "Sense-making " is a related term used by organizational behaviorists; sense-making reduces the world to a manageable cognitive package and helps groups perform effectively in unison. The shared story aligns action and belief. Interpreters hate counter-interpretation, which they correctly see as challenging their prestige and position. The successful entrepreneur of meaning, the sense-maker, accrues social prestige, however. The sense-maker is of course the supreme disambiguator.

Defining and Naming

Moderns exposed to the babble of mass communication sources may have a difficult time in stepping far enough back to regain (if indeed they ever once had) an abstract view of the power of definition and naming. There is also a tendency to confuse a name with the phenomenon under discussion. As Lippmann said, "First we define and then we see." Mere naming and description convey considerable power to manage an otherwise ambiguous reality. Definition conveys to some degree the power of management, which manifests as directed action in concert, e.g., defining something as a social stigma excludes undesirable(s) while reinforcing desired behaviors.

For a simple example, an "issue" may be "framed," such as "alcohol awareness," wherein drinking is defined as a social problem that requires administrative intervention. Such intervention may be required at many levels, for example by more police and law enforcement programs, the monitoring of drivers and college students, social programs, education, taxation, prevention (which knows no limits) or punishment. The frame justifies the actions and livelihoods of whole classes of administrators, and even casts them as heroic fighters against social sickness. University or school administrators may, for example, use such programs to show concern and to demonstrate the high moral purpose of "saving lives" and "bettering the human condition." Next month, however, the issue might be breast cancer or the Swine Flu. There is generally little or no meaningful follow-through on such programmatic issues because their de facto purpose is continual enhancement of the social standing of administrators. Program objectives are secondary, if even that.

Also, regarding definitions and nomenclature, consider the differing implications of the meanings of historical phrases such as *the Negro problem* versus *Black Power*, or *nigger* versus *African American*. The first term of each couplet implies, if not invites, a clinical or administrative solution, while the second term in each connotes self-direction, freedom and dignity. The Nazis used terms such as "Jewish bacillus" to define the Jews into extermination.[60] Once Jews were administratively defined into the "parasitic nation of Judea," it wasn't even necessary to suggest genocide — for this was the obvious, virtually automatic conclusion that flowed out of the definition — for what else is to be done about an infestation but extermination? Beware the implications of clinical metaphors in politics, for a power relationship is implied thereby.[61]

Euphemisms and dysphemisms disambiguate by moving things in or out of an interpretive forbidden zone. They roll off the modern corporate tongue for any occasion. The third quarter loss becomes a period of negative growth; the stock-market disaster, a market correction; the ignominious retreat, a re-deployment; mass firing is reorganization. There is no end to these games of self-serving simplification.

Official bureaucratic nomenclature carries connotations and implications that uncoil like a tightly wound spring. While the use of this sort of language to disambiguate might seem the most obvious thing in the world, it probably does not seem so obvious to those who, because of all-too-human time and energy constraints, take the way of least resistance by accepting official terminologies at face value. The drug problem, the health care problem, gun violence, the economy, preventions and clinical interventions concerning a host of problems, the public option, gun show loopholes: such terms fertilize administrative propagandas. The solutions of course tend to point in the direction of additional control by those using the nomenclature. The propagandist defines and conquers. The world simplifies into a clear problem/solution format that requires his special organizational remedy.[62]

---

60 Haig A. Bosmajian, *The Language of Oppression* (Washington: Public Affairs Press, 1974). This highly readable treatment discusses how language has been destructively aimed at Native Americans, Jews and Blacks.

61 See Michel Foucault, *Birth of the Clinic: An Archaeology of Medical Perception* (New York: Pantheon Books, 1973).

62 Some crank, or it may have been Thomas Szasz, observed that every new law creates a new class of criminals.

Agitation Propaganda

Agitation Propaganda, also called *agitprop*, polarizes, differentiates and disintegrates a preexisting, more or less stable social arrangement. A very important subspecies of disambiguation, it cleaves complicated social reality into a melodramatic, dichotomous struggle between victims (especially the victim-advocates and propagandists who claim to speak for the victims) and their oppressors. Aimed at promoting class warfare, division and tension, it splits asunder by exploiting extant social fault lines. Agitprop has been broadly useful in popular revolutionary propaganda because it is relatively easy to manufacture from common grievances. It has achieved its end when it has polarized people into camps and created an unstable social situation that can be exploited by the "agitators." It deliberately makes its target population angry over undeserved injustice(s), often presented in loving detail, stimulating resent and dissatisfaction with their lot under the current status quo (or what is claimed as the status quo) — e.g., "men have always exploited women both as sex objects and domestic slaves, sisters unite for equality!" Agitprop encourages people to feel and often behave like protagonists in a historical melodrama. Once the subjects have achieved a cohesive "solidarity," a term popular in agitprop, the highly excited mass suggestibility common to the mob makes them more easily herded by their propagandists.[63] As opposed to the apathetic or the contented, the polarized are relatively easy to align in common cause. A well-known principle in agitation propaganda and mob psychology is that a small cell of perhaps three or four "organizers" working in coordination can control and direct a very large mob or group once it has reached an excited state. Only an excited crowd will storm the barricades. It is the goal of agitprop to excite them. They become manageable precisely because an elemental worldview has been revealed to them in a very specific, unambiguous way. For instance, one already knows, pretty much, what the average unionist or feminist, products of agitation propaganda, will have to say on a given subject without the bother of having to ask. If agitation is couched in terms of sexism or unfair labor practices, they will likely picket, write letters, call in the civil rights commission or the

---

63 See Gustave Le Bon's *The Crowd: A Study of the Popular Mind* (New York: Macmillan Co., 1896).

board of labor practices, riot, shrilly protest, boycott, litigate or support litigation, give of their money or time, and at the very least will feel morally superior in a self righteous way and let all within earshot know it. Agitprop disambiguates the world into haves and have-nots, the justly deserving and the unjust, into a good-versus-evil morality play set in the backdrop of "political economy" or "social justice" in which the starring roles go to the aggrieved victims of injustice and the romantic heroes and heroines in "the struggle." Agitprop also has the salutary effect of focusing its target population, making them feel more efficacious as human beings by identifying combatable causes of unhappiness. Thus it remedies meaninglessness and focuses energies that might be dissipated in despair. Practitioners of agitprop are sometimes called "organizers."

Agitprop has a proven track record where disparities or simple differences exist between rich and poor, black and white, men and women, proletariat and capitalist, colonized and colonizer, rural and urban, labor and management, faculty and administration. Best yet, from the propagandist's perspective, because agitprop can be generally created out of garden-variety thematic materials, it is a low capital, low-tech enterprise. Agitprop is often delivered via rhetoric of racism, sexism, class or ethnic hatred, grievances or injustices. Ellul believed it works especially well on the illiterate and uneducated, in contrast to other types of propaganda that so thoroughly informed the educated mind. My observation, however, is that the "educated" are just as vulnerable if not more so; many humanities and social science professors seem to be totally in the grips of agitation propaganda; of course, it could be that standards for professorships have declined since Ellul's time.

Always revolutionary, agitprop promotes "the struggle;" it is an accelerant of social combustion. The disambiguating sociology that underlies Marxism, as far as most adherents seemingly understand it, for example, is in abstract merely the Robin Hood tale adjusted to agitate. It features a historical made-for-TV class struggle. A wealthy upper class, owning the means of production, oppresses the proletariat yeomen, merry men and women who live in a natural socialistic state in the Sherwood Forest of revolutionary commune. It's all there in the *Communist Manifesto*, which is as neat a piece of disambiguating agitation, an historical romance, as has ever been written. Once understood, the direction of action becomes obvious. Lenin's apt metaphor for the movement for international communism was of innumerable droplets of outrage all combining into a flood.

Social movements in the technical, formal sense of identity-driven politics depend upon agitation propaganda to generate mass power. Even though on the surface there may seem to be many different kinds of agitprop, the basic idea is always the same: some preexisting grievance or schism is selected and irritated to the point of inflammation. The union organizer bemoans the injustices and greed of "management" for paying themselves huge bonuses in bad times while laying off workers whom it has been exploiting all along anyway. In much the same way, the radical feminist denounces the *phallogocentrism* — the penis-centered logic of the patriarchal world — behind women's exploitation, unequal pay, glass ceilings, sexism, domestic violence and commercial exploitation of women who are treated as mere sex objects, insecure consumers, chattel or emotion-driven hysterics.[64]

Cartoon Histories and Cosmologies

Naïve people talk about "history" as if there were a single objectively true standard edition lying about somewhere on a shelf. Maybe this is true, and we would all like to find that lost volume, but in propaganda the purpose of history is to control the present and the future. History does not take place in the past but in the present. If you peruse old books, you may have noticed how poorly most historical treatments age — a history written in past decades, with few exceptions, often reads like value-laden ranting. Any public version of history is essentially propaganda,[65] falling quickly into myth, and may have little or nothing to do with history per se as a record of what happened or allegedly happened. History instead becomes a disambiguating story

---

64 The word "hysterical" literally indicates a wandering womb, a source of feminine disorders that could only have been thought of by a man. The idea was that the womb got loose of its moorings somehow and wandered around the body, causing otherwise unaccountable disorders such as hysterical blindness. The cure was a good man and an adult state of sexual development. The proper sexual order of things cured. See Luce Iragaray's "This Sex Which is Not One" for an essay on how female sexuality has been conceptualized by Freud and other men.

65 See George Orwell's *1984*, which Anthony Burgess, in Burgess's *1985* explains was really written about 1948 not 1984; Orwell's editor made him change it. Orwell demonstrates an absolutely fluid use of history in state propaganda.

that crudely imparts moral/ethical lessons. I offer several generalized examples.

Consider the old cartoon version of American history — the one informing the *Leave it to Beaver* era — that socialized generations through the 1960s. It goes something like this: *A bunch of white men arrive at Plymouth Rock and the delighted Indians treat them to a Thanksgiving dinner. Following "manifest destiny," they civilize the wilderness, reject old King George, and bring order, liberty and political representation for all. After crossing the Delaware, cutting the cherry tree and being placed on the dollar bill, George Washington becomes a symbol of order and economic free market power. Davy Crockett, Daniel Boone and John Wayne conquer the West, and die heroically at the Alamo. John Wayne, resurrected, defeats the Indians and the Japanese who sneak-attacked Pearl Harbor, and pulls off D-Day. The result is safety, baseball, electrification, continued freedom to suburbia, as long as Communism is resisted and the American Way (business) thrives.* Except for perhaps a few details, this is the essential cartoon history of at least a generation. History books consisted of the exploits and contests of white men such as Thomas Edison with an occasional, rare guest appearance from Betsy Ross.

Then there is a new cartoon history that has emerged since about 1970. As told in the American public schools, it goes something like this: *Ethnocentric White Anglo-Saxon Protestant men arrived in the new world importing slavery, disease and also bringing death and dislocation to the culturally superior, environmentally conscious indigenous peoples who were not entrained to the same "linear" conceptualization of progress as the white man. The Civil War was then fought to free the black slaves, subsequently oppressed by racism until Dr. Martin Luther King Jr. led the Civil Rights Movement. Despite all this oppression, black men and women invented the traffic light, discovered blood plasma and jazz, George Washington Carver harnessed the power of the peanut, Beethoven was black, as were the Pharaohs. Blacks built the pyramids, not as slaves but as architects and occupants. Sometime between the Civil War and the Civil Rights Movement, World War II was fought because of the Holocaust, and won by the Tuskegee Airman and the contributions of women who flew airplanes and left their homes and roles as housewives to work in the war factories, where they were often subjected to severe sexual harassment and race-gender discrimination. The contributions of women and Native Americans were systematically ignored by the*

WASPs, but now cultural diversity reigns and will be institutionalized forever in social and educational services, and in innumerable urban boulevards and high schools named after Dr. King and Rosa Parks, who was too tired to go to the back of the bus. This amalgam is a blend of the women's history movement and the black studies movement. Expressed doubt is treated like heresy in some current university settings. Vague allusions to cultural diversity have now kept a generation of administrators on their feet, themselves in nowise "diverse," or at best nominally diverse, and for whom it provides a higher reason to draw higher pay while spouting platitudes. The extreme ends of the modern Democratic and Republican parties merely carry forward variations of these two histories.

Continuing such examples, women's history, "Herstory," a dreadful pun that is not always intended as a pun, becomes in its cartoon version a tale of the Civilizing Woman, variously told, who invents agriculture. Humans were originally, naturally matriarchal, with worship of the Goddess evidenced in the Stone Age Venuses, those squat pot-bellied female figures that turn up regularly at European archeological digs. Descent was reckoned matrilinearly under the old natural female order, for who could really know who was the father? Motherhood, however, is as unambiguous as one can get — e.g., Mother Earth and Mother Russia, and is the source of all life. "Thealogy," Goddess study, is the proper name for patriarchy's "theology," the study of God. Under patriarchy the image of the Goddess has been corrupted and transgendered into a white-bearded old man. The tale of the Garden of Eden is an analogy of how rising Patriarchy attacked and subjugated primal Women's religion. The tree and the snake in Genesis were the symbols of the old Women's Religion, of its fertile knowledge and wisdom, to which Judaism and Christianity, both patriarchal male-god religions, attached slanderous connotations. Women became, under the Judeo-Christian tradition and in Freudian psychology — which merely carries on the prudery and women-oppression of the patriarchal tradition — temptresses, hysterics and repositories of lewd sexuality and carnal knowledge. Their lips were smoother than oil. The true knowledge of woman's powerful wisdom was systematically suppressed — as when male heirs literally erased the lithoglyphs of Hatshepsu (variously spelled), Egypt's female Pharaoh — a process that has continued throughout western history and also with the subjection of women in the

Church.[66] The "Womyn's Movement" will set all this right, all the sooner once it eliminates gender-biased language and pronouns in English composition classes. Woe to the college fresh-person who uses gender-biased pronouns.

Here is yet another: the Nazi-Aryan historical cartoon. Higher culture is a product of the Aryan Race. This is the civilizing race that invented mathematics, logic, science, music, physics, higher art, architecture, medicine and so forth. Seen as both a race and language group, Aryan man is represented by the unending procession of notable figures and geniuses of the human race — the classical Greeks and Romans, composers, pioneers, literary figures, philosophers and scientists. Lesser races merely muddle along, degenerate, some at the expense of Aryan Man — e.g., the Jews, who are parasites, and the Slavs, who are sub-human *Untermenschen*. Racial purity matters because History unfolds as the march of the high race hindered by the low. Neo-Nazis and Christian Identity churches of white supremacists merely add some variations to this story, e.g., Jesus was blond with blue eyes.

Black Muslims disambiguate a hard world with a history/cosmology of a black scientist, Yakub, living on the moon, who in the course of his work thousands of years ago created the white, blue-eyed devil, the results from scientific research gone wrong. The blue-eyed devil subsequently enslaved the black man and has afflicted him ever since.

The historical cartoon that informs communism, already mentioned, operates in some ways like the old Nordic Wyrd — Fate, inescapable. Its conception of dialectical historical progress predestines the revolutionary social movement that ultimately arrives at Communism. This process is as predictable as the tides, so woe betides the counter-revolutionary who through his thoughts and actions writes himself out of historical progress. The propagandist in this situation merely has to call "all aboard" for the train of history.[67]

Even Judaism, speaking secularly, possibly owes its continuing existence through the ages to the strength of a great story. The Jews are the chosen people. They have a pact with God. There is more to the

66 A formerly Catholic woman told me of having met with her parish priest for counseling concerning her marriage to an abusive and adulterous husband. In essence, she said, the counsel she received was to go home, cook dinner and spread her legs.

67 This metaphor belongs to Hannah Arendt from her *Origins of Totalitarianism* (New York: Meridian Books, 1958).

story, of course, but a deal is a deal. The compact strength of this tale has carried Judaism through the continents and the ages. Christianity is yet another great story: eternal salvation and deliverance from cold death in a package that a child or mass man/woman can grasp in an instant.

It seems unlikely there could be a mass movement without some such cartoon history, cosmology or sociology. Propaganda enters in when these explanations of existence are organizationally appropriated and used to benefit their tellers, which happens often. Eric Hoffer believed there were no true mass movements left in America because every movement quickly becomes a cult, a corporation or a scam.[68] That is to say, propagandists agilely appropriate true social movements for their own use.

Stories and Paradigms

By paradigms I mean broadly socially shared, vividly abstract cases or situations that serve as the common clarifying examples and "for instances" in everyday communication, e.g., paradigmatic stories, folklore, myths, so-called urban myths, examples, clichés, parables, stereotypes and anecdotes. Paradigms tend to be unquestioned or assumed in communication — and are commonly used as self-evident proofs, the things that everyone supposedly knows. There are too many such paradigms to attempt anything like a complete list, but a few common ones will be mentioned.

Scientism and Progress

Scientism is a religious belief in science — that science knows all, sees all, or is at least on its way to omniscience. This belief is almost universal in the West. Sometimes referred to as positivism, scientism comforts because of its promise of illuminating the darkness. Beyond doubt, science has eased many of the pains of life, although at what ultimate cost it is difficult to say; but this book is not a philosophic speculation on the unintended consequences of science. Science

---

68 See Hoffer's *The Temper of our Time: Essays* (New York: Harper & Row, 1967).

opposes superstition while Scientism is a superstitious belief in science. In this secular Western administrative age, Science and Progress have been woven together as a ceremonial mantle worn by elites, who, in the West, are no longer able to justify themselves as earthly representatives of God. They now must show themselves as enlightened, democratic representatives applying objective principles of scientific management to human problems. In actual practice, however, weakly supported hypothetical scientistic conjectures are applied as absolutes to justify decisions. Of course, the trained scientist well knows the provisional nature of much scientific theory; but such people are few. Propagandists stretch beyond reason the qualified nuances of the scientists. The theory of global warming, whatever its true merits, increasingly appears to have been used as cartoon or pseudo science in this way. In the field of education, highly tentative theories of pedagogy have been used to justify a system of mass education that appears more and more designed to benefit its administrators and its political champions than its ostensible subjects.[69] Science is used as an ultimate disambiguator: "Science tells us that we must do X," say the elites, thereby prescribing a plan, their plan, for action.

Any number of paradigms are related to work: the intrinsic benefit of working your way up from the bottom, from so-called humble origins; the rather amazing notion that "working your way through college" is good for a person when all it generally does is blunt effort, sensibilities and prevents the campus involvement that is an essential part of the college experience; or that businessmen necessarily know how to run a country, university or, nowadays, even a business. So useful are such stories that political candidates package themselves to disguise their true class origins and simulate the hard-working character that so much separates the moral wheat from the chaff. For example, a few years ago during the George W. Bush versus Al Gore presidential election, both candidates appeared in contrived news events pretending to be the "salt of the earth." Bush wore shit-kicker, down-on-the-ranch clothing in Texas, while Gore pretended to split wood down on the Tennessee farm, dressed ridiculously for the occasion in white

---

69 The rise of education colleges has accompanied the decline of literacy — and since the latter is required to become truly educated — what C. Wright Mills called "self-educating," — this decline may be the tragedy of our times. The results have been to ensconce educators while limiting knowledge acquirement of those who must suffer under the curriculum.

slacks and a polo shirt. Yet both are equally products of the same elite schools and social milieu.

Visual, Graphics, Film and "Docugandas"

A premium means of disambiguation in modern informational sociology is by what are sometimes called "good visuals," by which I refer to little vignettes set up for the purpose of sending a summarized message to distant audience members whose attention span is likely measured in seconds. The good visual essentializes a story. More accurately, the visual *is* the story, for exposure to it is as far as most people will ever get along the path of knowledge. Political protesters must often attempt such vignettes, too, because it may be the only form of mass media coverage they can obtain, so compact explanation becomes paramount. Think of the classic Hallmark card: brief, to the point, "Mom, we love you," illustrated with flowers. No thought required.

A typical visual of this sort is the standard antiwar demonstration showing a hillside of white crosses, each representing a soldier killed. It is instantaneously comprehensible. Presidential propaganda is often conveyed via self-evident spectacles. A president, looking presidential, is shown surrounded by health care professionals, stethoscoped and smocked, touting his party's health care bill. When fear of crime is an opportune topic, uniformed law enforcement officers stand in, surrounding the President in the Oval Office. To summon up the Labor vote, he appears in the factory setting in rolled up shirtsleeves, praising the men and women of organized Labor who built this great country, even though one may doubt there has been a president in the past 100 years from whom one could get a good day's manual work. The classic anti-gun spectacle shows a wall of victims' photographs, or uniformed police and mayors with a table of dramatically ugly, and therefore highly telegenic "assault weapons." In all cases, a virtually self-evident story is conveyed, with time needed for comprehension, perhaps two seconds; a picture having a moral and a hero, namely the propagandist's cause. And yes, of course, such stories are gross oversimplifications, if not downright misleading, and are all the more so for having been seasoned with a few grains of fact. But disambiguation must be achieved if the message is not to overtax the sensibilities of the audience.

Even the global warming story has been codified into a now standard "B-roll" visual. B-rolls are those canned video clips that news producers keep on file for use as background to a news story narrative (the A-roll). The now standardized B-roll for the "global warming", "Climate-change" story shows glaciers and icebergs melting into the sea and polar bears swimming. The story decodes piteously: the ice is melting and those poor polar bears must swim for it.

Graphic simplifying visuals depicting polls and social indicators see similar use. Crime is up or down according to the bar graph, a story that both justifies extant programs and the need for more. There is the amusing example of Ronald Reagan, whose presidential addresses were sometimes set before stock-market type graphs that had no units on their vertical or horizontal axes, and not referred to in the address in any case. The charts were merely props for playing the role of the authoritative, scientifically informed executive. Or, using polling data, public opinion might be shown trending in some direction or other and must be satisfied as if it constituted absolute authority for whatever policy is being proposed. The term "mandate" is often used, even though assigning absolute meaning to survey data can be very chancy.

Docuganda results when the documentary film meets propaganda. Of course, a case can be made that film in general may be the greatest propaganda medium ever yet invented.[70] Think about it. The editor can select from raw video footage of hundreds of hours in length, footage of related or unrelated events, perhaps totally lacking in coherence, from various sources, and from it clip and juxtapose whatever images she wishes into a seamless story. Abetting this synthetic reality, sound/ music and a scripted narrative (preferably in a high-toned accent) may create virtually any impression desired. The documentary film is a genre that lends itself to extreme disambiguation. Things that do not necessarily go together, through the miracle of editing, narrative and sound, appear attached and coherent. In the final edited form, all this goes by so quickly that few in the intended audiences are able take a step back, perceptually, to consider how the editor arbitrarily makes connections, for there are no accidents in editing. Of course what is said here applies to film, newscasts, entertainment, as well as documentary. The story takes on a life of its own quite separate from actual

---

70 Although this idea should be self-evident to a thoughtful person, the notion that film is the best yet propaganda medium is by no means my idea, but I cannot provide a source.

events. The adage applied to news writing applies equally well to film or docuganda: *never let the facts get in the way of a good story*. People want and need the sort of clarity delivered by disambiguation because it saves them mental work and resolves the anxiety consequent to too much ambiguity. As particularly vivid examples, I mention a few famous docuganda films that have served to disambiguate. *The Eternal Jew*, directed by Fritz Hippler, made a long-winded but easily understandable case that the Jews were parasites that fed off the creative work of host nations. *Triumph of the Will* by Leni Riefenstahl shows the 1934 Nazi Party rally in Nuremberg as a German Renaissance, the fusion of hard work, inspiration, leadership and pride that has set the Reich back on the path of destiny. Frank Capra's *Know Your Enemy: Japan*, the very same director that made the Christmas favorite *It's a Wonderful Life*, indicts the Japanese for crushing the little guy, the all important individual citizen of American democracy, in favor of a war machine that promoted conformity with mad doctrines made by a few big wigs. In doing this, Capra simply inverts the basic theme of his popular films — the little guy matters, especially in the mythos of American democracy. I recommend viewing these films because they so well exemplify how high contrast disambiguation has been achieved for particular audiences; they also are easy to find and view online; and there is no substitute for seeing for one's self.

A story in all the above cases is created largely through juxtaposition, the arbitrary placing/editing of material in proximity to suggest association; use of background music/noise suggesting some effect — evil, chaotic, exotic, ridiculous — lots of possibilities exist here; and a narrative line that is carried either by dialogue, a voiceover narrator or animated cartoon graphics. The basic story in each is extremely simple, which contributes to the films' power.

An interesting property of images, sounds and juxtaposition is that, in a manner of speaking, they lie beyond truth or falsity. An image or a sound is merely what it is and suggests what it suggests, but advances no claim that can be logically refuted. The images shown to any target population are very carefully selected while innumerable other images are rejected and "left on the cutting room floor." There are no accidents. The audience member then goes even further by fusing the ideas in his head, as humans will do, and projecting into the film even more coherence than the editor was able to suggest.

In *Know Your Enemy: Japan,* Frank Capra applied the same film-making genius to propaganda that he used to create many of the immensely popular, moneymaking films of his time. He explained the need for fighting to the American soldiers of the Pacific Theater, who in 1945 seemed about to face their bloodiest confrontations yet in the war. This film was essentially aimed at soldiers and a public that would be sustaining the war effort. My father saw the film while soldiering on Okinawa, and remembered parts of it quite well, many years later. This screening took place when the island was being used as a marshalling point for the imminent invasion of Japan. It was unclear at that time if the Japanese would ever surrender; if anything, surrender seemed most unlikely. The atomic bomb was a secret known to a few, unknown to the masses and soldiers, and yet untested in war.[71] It seemed the U.S. would have to invade the Japanese mainland to finish the war, an invasion that could have resulted in millions of civilian and military casualties. Considering a propensity for Japanese soldiers to fight to the death, commit suicide or sacrifice themselves, and the levels of social control and organization of the Japanese civilian population, the greatest bloodshed appeared yet to come. Since the average person does not kill unless pushed to extremes, a motivating and totally clear explanation was needed for those about to undertake what seemed sure to be grim business.

Know Your Enemy: Japan provides this much-needed explanation. The genius of the film is in its editing. Capra used bits and pieces from dozens of other films and newsreels, including Japanese propaganda films, historical dramas, travel logs and public health footage. Parts are infused with anthropological flavor, examining the state religion that obligates the Japanese to serve the Emperor unto death. Other parts are more historical. Capra clipped and edited these fragments, added a narration with the radio-newscaster inflection of urgency, and used some Disney-like animation as connecting tissue, showing a Japanese octopus stabbing its dagger as it moved to assault the eight corners of the world. Japanese generals and political figures are quoted with

---

71 My father said that just before the atomic bomb was dropped, which he and his fellow soldiers on Okinawa knew nothing about until afterward, orders went out that they all were to equip themselves with gasmasks and full field kits. The generals apparently believed that the Japanese would retaliate with whatever they had, including poison gas.

cartoon-accents exactly like those used when Popeye the Sailor fights Japanese submarines in the feature cartoons that were being shown at the movie houses of the era. Japanese soldiers are said to be as alike as two prints from the same photographic negative.

Capra knew how to tell a story. In what might be one of the best segments of film propaganda ever made, perhaps three minutes in length, he shows how the Japanese soldier is developed from the child. A mechanical steel forge, many tons in weight, pounds a billet of almost white hot metal into shape, sparks flying, whump, whump, whump, which together with an frantic orchestral scherzo achieves a headachy cacophony. This steely heartbeat rhythmically underlies a series of rapidly changing clips of Japanese children in kendo practice and other physical fitness activities; eerie clips of perhaps two seconds length of children in goggles walk in line before X-ray machines, replete with crackling electrical noises; children rote-learning by collectively reciting lessons in classrooms. The clips move on to the training of soldiers, charging, bayoneting, and end with the full profile of the Japanese soldier, who after having had all the humanity burned out of him, as in the manufacture of steel, says the narrator in that radio news voice, is now ready to burn, slash and stab his way across the world to enforce Japanese racial supremacy. "Made In Japan" rubber-stamps the end of the segment.

The film overwhelms with the amount of information conveyed, yet at the same time, the story itself is so simple that anyone would understand and retain it: as a general impression the Japanese were dangerous single-minded humans and would have to be dealt with accordingly, like it or not. Not only is this point made as unambiguously as it can be, note, too, how well the segment satisfies the Second Commandment of Propaganda concerning reflected values — the Japanese are condemned for violating that central American value of the intrinsic worth of the individual, the little guy. Propaganda permits no grey areas.

More modern docuganda differs only by moving at a faster pace. *Know Your Enemy: Japan* lasts for well over an hour and amounts to a serious, fact-filled lecture that is far too taxing for today's attention-deficit mass audiences, even though molding a general impression was probably all that was needed for the film to have its desired effect. Today's films also differ by being more reliant on irony rather than a straight serious lecture — for example, see how any of Michael Moore's documentary films are constructed.[72]

Disambiguate. Effective propaganda tells a simple story.

---

72 I know of no way of neatly separating the propaganda film from the entertainment film or the documentary from the docuganda, other than by the more or less obvious earmarks of the genre. Films of all sorts have been vehicles for propaganda.

The Fourth Commandment

USE GROUP PRESSURE TO HORIZONTALLY SHAPE BELIEFS AND BEHAVIOR

The modern trend in propaganda has been toward managing individuals by means of group pressure. This may surprise many who conceive of propaganda in its more obvious forms, the traditional vertical, top down information flow as represented by political speeches, films, posters and mass news-entertainment media.

But group-level, so-called *horizontal propaganda* is perhaps the most effective way yet devised of inducing conformity, belief and desired behavior in a target population.[73] The basic idea behind

---

73 The terms "horizontal propaganda" and "vertical propaganda" belong to Jacques Ellul, who had much to say on the use of groups in the Maoist propaganda of the communist Chinese revolution. Horizontal propaganda was also fundamental to the implementation of the Communist Revolution in the old Soviet Union, where there were study groups for everyone and committees, always committees, at every level of society. Of course, both of these states became nations of informers as well, where even non-enthusiasm was regarded as a serious nonconformity and could be punished by death or exile that often led to death — in Siberia or elsewhere.

horizontal propaganda is that the average human, by nature a social animal, will align with the normative pressures of the group in which he is placed or trapped, as in a school, institutional or work situation. Importantly, to propagandists, such groups perform reasonably well at modifying behavior, which is a far more difficult undertaking than merely changing, installing or refocusing attitudes or beliefs by means of the old vertical "educational" propagandas.[74] Even more importantly, perhaps, such groups help construct shared interpretations of reality that benefit those who set up and facilitate such groups. Here, the propagandist contrives a new informational sociology at a basic social level. It's called "horizontal" because the pressure to conform comes from all sides, from peers, rather than merely from above.

Horizontal propaganda increasingly permeates the corporate and political worlds in America and elsewhere. Utilizing mainly small groups, it operates under innocuous names such as team management, democratization of the workplace, taking ownership of the job, quality circles, shared governance, employee participation, and many others.[75] It extends, supplements, complements, and replaces, with a superior technique, the vertical reporting lines of informational control typical of the centralized, authoritative bureaucracy. It differs fundamentally from the social interpretation style and dynamics of truly autonomous independent groups in that goals, ideology and fundamental social orientation are inserted from above or trifled with by authority; it is also very easily confused with the genuine, autonomous groups characteristic of true democratic self-governance, of which it is merely a pseudomorph. Managerial manipulators disguise it as shared governance, and may themselves be confused or clueless as to what true democracy really is and is not. The attempt is to make the subject complicit in his own binding. These attempts often work.

---

74 To illustrate the difference between attitude change (or installation) and behavior change, take the example of the smoker. The smoker knows smoking is bad for him; all sorts of information/beliefs have been installed in him to this effect by top-down communication campaigns. Yet he still smokes. The best way to get him to stop is to put him in a support group or group therapy where group norms come into play.

75 Barker wrote a wonderful case study of a manufacturing plant that converted from bureaucratic to team management. "Tightening the Iron Cage: Concertive Control in Self-Managing Teams" (*Administrative Science Quarterly* Vol. 38, No. 3, September 1993). Barker now teaches at the U.S. Air Force Academy, which suggests the direct military and organizational applications of much group management theory.

Groups are pressure-cookers of conformity. Simply through the action of placing a person in an organizationally-created group or team situation, where everyone in the group communicates, relies upon and is known to one another, a dozen or more peer-supervisors replace the sole supervisor that is used in traditional top-down forms of organization. Everyone in the group now finds himself accountable to his coworkers, "the team."

Under the old top-down systems, a subordinate can easily tell, or imagine telling the boss to bugger off (or manifest this feeling via passive aggression); but this is not so easily managed with peers, who must be relied upon for support, social and otherwise, and an assured place on the team. So instead of just one supervisor and a fixed job description that lays out terms and conditions that contractually delimit the bureaucratic system and its relationship with the individual, the individual is now tied into a complicated, open-ended, ever-evolving network of performance expectations in which he finds himself ever more at a loss. Outnumbered, structurally disadvantaged, socially outmaneuvered, outweighed, the defense of "that's not my job," becomes an irrelevant if not outright deviant utterance: one can't let down the group. While still remaining *sub-ordinate*, as the old vertical lines of authority seldom disappear although they may become less visible, the hapless subject becomes *co-ordinate* as well. A whole new dimension of social controls has been added. One hears the term, "the commitment organization."

Furthermore, there is an even more amazing aspect of such groups. Much evidence shows that the group experience distorts the perceptions of reality held by group members. Those who align with group pressure perceive or misperceive the outside world as group consciousness would have it seen. To a fairly large extent, groups create their own social realities, using their own sense-making[76] schemes to explain the universe, a fact having huge implications.

A few classic, well-known social psychology experiments illustrate the power of groups on reality perception. In Solomon Asch's "lines" experiment, still replicated in some high school social studies classes, a naïve subject placed in a group situation is asked to judge the relative length of a set of lines by selecting the longest. The experiment

---

76 See Karl Weick on group/organizational sense-making, ponderous armchair philosopher that he may be: *Sensemaking in Organizations* (Thousand Oaks, CA: Sage, 1995).

is rigged. When the subject names the truly longest line, the rest of the group, confederates of the experimenter, selects another visibly shorter line. The subject is thus placed in the uncomfortable situation of being directly at odds with a strong group, "public" opinion. Understandably, subjects are perplexed. But most, after a few repetitions, begin to go along with the group. Of course many are just faking it, avoiding conflict. And why should they not, for what advantage is there to arguing with an ad hoc group from which they will soon be walking away? Interviewed afterward, away from the group, some continued to give the incorrect "group" answer. They actually appeared to believe a shorter line was longest, and somehow aligned their perceptions with the group norm. Now, if a transitory experience in an ad hoc group can produce this sort of lasting perception, a distorted reality, then how much greater must be the effects of group pressure on individuals in real life group settings from which they cannot escape so easily, e.g., social institutions, cults, jobs, professions, administrative regimes and other voluntary or involuntary associations?[77]

Another study, fabulous in its power and simplicity, is Kurt Lewin's organ meats experiment. As part of the general rationing program during World War II, American authorities attempted to convince housewives to purchase organ meats such as liver, hearts and kidneys to feed their families, thereby leaving the better, more expensive cuts of meats for distribution to the millions of men in armed services. It was relatively easy to "educate" housewives about the many nutritional, economic and patriotic benefits of organ meats. But merely possessing this information did not translate into the behavior of consumption, for measurable attitude change does not necessarily equal behavior change. The "educated" housewives still avoided organ meats. In an attempt at behavior change, Lewin ingenuously placed housewives on committees and charged them with the task of finding a solution to the problem of how to get housewives to buy organ meats. Both attitude and behavior change then followed. One might attribute this change to so-called "taking ownership," or a need for behavioral consistency or rationalization for having participated in the group, or cognitive dissonance, or any number of fashionable management

---

77 This question echoes a concern of the great social psychologist Stanley Milgram, who in construing the meaning of his famous obedience experiments, worried that human nature was insufficient to protect us from the destructive effects of unscrupulous authority.

or social-psychological theories. Much explanatory jargon has been generated concerning such group phenomena. Attribute the change to whatever psychological mechanism you will, but these horizontal techniques are often effective. Many modern corporate environments, e.g., universities, now employ such means.

Anyone who has ever attended a DARE (Drug Addiction Resistance Education) session as a child or teenager in an American school since about the 1970s has been exposed to a type of this group manipulation. Role-playing (done in a group) is a classic horizontal propaganda technique. In DARE, youthful participants act out the situation of being approached by a drug pusher and refusing the offer. Similar manipulations are often used by social workers. I recollect one community health program that used role-playing to teach crack whores how to negotiate condom use on the part of their clients so as to minimize AIDS transmission. Therapy groups are another common application used to create and reinforce new behaviors.

Several principals apply to propaganda via horizontal methods, although probably no one understands all there is to know about group propaganda, for like all complicated social phenomena, murk and mystery are always present to some degree. Groups often try to impose absolute interpretations of reality on their members, and upon anyone else they are able to dominate, demanding conformity in thought and deed in any number of ways. Groups are also well-known for driving out or marginalizing deviates, even though such deviations may be very subtle as seen from the outside. It is also generally thought that for such groups to be most effective at creating behavior they must be what are called primary groups. These are the important groups that one must depend upon for social or economic support and often for life itself: a combat team, the family, a professional team with built-in incentives for career success, an urban street gang which may substitute for lack of a functional family and other social support.

From the moment they form, groups begin to manifest what is generally called in-group/out-group bias. The "in-group" sees itself as superior, morally and otherwise, to "out-groups," and will selectively interpret reality to maintain such beliefs. It fosters an interior social reality. This may manifest explicitly or implicitly. The concept of "groupthink" was once popular to explain some of the more fantastic errors of collective judgment that such interior-group realities may create.[78] While there is possibly such a thing as collective wisdom, having occasionally witnessed it myself, much hard evidence also supports the existence of collective stupidity, e.g., the fixed super-fortifications of the Maginot Line that were supposed to protect France from German invasion. This massive national defense project was tactically obsolete even before construction began.

Groups often have powerful behavioral effects: members will dress, speak, and act differently after becoming caught up in the group. Sometimes this process of creation may be called team spirit; those who can help create and direct it may be well rewarded, and it may reward group members as well — e.g., a successful sports or sales team. Sometimes, however, groups may create belief systems that put them so much at odds with society and external reality as to result in the destruction of the group. Consider small groups of radical militia members who in the 1990s conspired to blow up expressway bridges in Michigan so as to somehow save America from invasion by United Nations troops. Only intense group dynamics can create and maintain such a fantastical shared interpretation of reality. Viewed from the outside, it is difficult to imagine the process by which militia members arrived at this "truth," but be assured that from an interior perspective, it all made perfect sense.

Such dynamics also explain why executive/corporate cultures are at times capable of such astonishing idiocies — assuming their continual funding with other people's money — for they spend much of their time closeted with one another in meetings that functionally resemble echo chambers. An inward-looking, self-reinforcing group dynamic comes to rule them. Deviance is not acceptable and may not even be safely voiced. It comes to be seen as irrational or obstructionist. Cults have similar effects on members, and what the difference may be between a cult and any particular executive culture group or board of directors is not always clear. But if a cult can convince highly educated members to castrate themselves and dress alike while expecting a space ship to take them to a better world, as with the Heaven's Gate Cult whose members committed mass suicide in California in 1997, an executive culture can certainly convince its inhabitants that mediocrity and vapid imitation embody "excellence."

---

78 The name *groupthink* originates with Irving Janis, who cataloged eight indicators or symptoms of the groupthink syndrome.

I once investigated the source of cult-like chanting at a convention center. My ears led me to a meeting room that held a wildly loud group of perhaps 50 people. Observing, at first the event seemed to be a religious revival meeting of the primitive sort, where those who "get the spirit" may speak in tongues and start dancing or rolling around on the floor (hence the term "Holy Rollers"). However, it turned out to be an inspirational sales meeting for employees of a door-to-door vacuum cleaner company. Such intense groups dynamics might be the only way to steel door-to-door vacuum sales people to sustain themselves in the world of "no" through which they must pass to obtain each single sale.

Other sales programs are often conducted via the group — the Tupperware Party, but also lingerie parties and even sex toy purveyors set up group events in which social pressure can play to their advantage. So-called network marketing entrains individuals into groups. The old "Amway Ambush" relies on a small group setting in which to pressure the outnumbered and outmaneuvered individual. Typically, the subject is invited to the home of a former acquaintance, who has been recruited in the network marketing scheme unbeknownst to the subject, and pressed to buy in an intense, scripted small group setting in which the subject is very much at a disadvantage.

Primitive type groups are to be found still in modern corporate and organizational settings. So-called *basic assumption groups*[79] take the form of *fight/flight groups*, the unspoken assumption being exactly as the name suggests; *messianic groups* organized around a strong charismatic leader in which the basic assumption is personal advancement or protection through worship of or servitude to the strong one, and *pairing groups* that exist to bond and unite. Despite ostensible high purposes and a modern corporate environment, many groups are forever limited by such primitive dynamics. They are never able to overcome the dynamic to accomplish usefully creative work in concert, such creative work being an achievement that is perhaps too sophisticated, beyond the psychological developmental scope of many

---

79 Wilfred Bion describes basic assumption groups in his *Experiences with Groups* (London: Tavistock, 1959). He formulated these ideas while conducting group therapy sessions in military hospitals. These assumptions, in operation, essentially delimit many groups, confining them to a primitive developmental stage. Bion spent much time in running so called T-groups, therapy groups.

people, and which exceeds their skills in group settings (which must be painfully learned).

Another strand of thought related to horizontal propaganda, a very influential strand, deals with larger groups such as crowds and mobs — also extending to mass media audiences, which share many characteristics with crowds. Crowds tend toward irrational, extreme or even violent behavior that generally involves various distortions of reality. Crowds are highly suggestible, as are the individuals comprising them, who seem to experience a collective mind. But this mind seemingly is of a primitive animalistic type. Crowds and mobs do not generally bring out the best in people, but rather the worst. Crowds may go from maudlin sentimentality to lynch mob viciousness in moments, i.e., *mass hysteria.*

Something about the experience of being in a crowd or group makes the individual feel less accountable for his actions and less moored to day-to-day behavioral norms. The saying is "alone in the crowd" because crowds create a cloud of invisibility for the individual, who effectively disappears in it.[80] And how many times do people, especially younger people, who tend anyway toward geniality and malleability from peer influence,[81] find themselves in a group and "carried away?" They may commit acts that they would never have considered when alone, in a presumably more rational state of mind. Of course higher brain functions flood back if the person later finds himself quite visibly alone in jail.[82]

Propagandists have long understood that people are usually more deeply and readily persuadable when in crowds. Hence the political rally or the presidential visit as a fixture in politics, where the charismatic leader excites the mass individual, who is not at all the same man or woman as the rational solitary individual, even though both inhabit the same body. The excitement of the crowd washes over and

---

80 If one really wishes to disappear, then one must go to the big city where anonymity and solitude in the midst of the uncaring millions is possible. In the small towns and countryside, everyone too soon knows you and your business.

81 This is basic Aristotle, the second book of *Rhetoric*, in which he describes the character of Youth; among its traits is an excessive congeniality.

82 Chris Matthews, graduate student and documentary filmmaker, witnessed recent Toledo riots resulting when Neo-Nazis staged a deliberatively provocative demonstration in a largely black neighborhood. He knew of young men who, caught up in the crowd frenzy, unplanned, did things that landed them in state prison for eight-year terms (personal communication, January 2010).

erodes the critical faculties of the individual. He is transported away from himself.

It is also well-known to agitation propagandists and similar "community organizers" that a small cell of three or four people can, by prearranged plan, control and direct a crowd of hundreds. I have seen this happen, where just a few teenagers working together directed a crowd of several hundred of their peers to attack their high school. The situation was already polarized, a crowd had gathered largely because of curiosity over a demonstration. Very little effort was required to steer various individuals in the crowd: the excitement of chanting in unison was followed by a suggestion here, a direction there, urging an apparently drunken young man to take up and throw a barricade through a window, another to pull a fire alarm. Others followed these "leaders," who were really puppets; things quickly escalated and the resulting bedlam, and fear of more vandalism, which included throwing benches through plate glass windows behind which the school's officials were standing, closed the school for days.

Nazism in Germany must in some large part be understood as a group propaganda phenomenon, as were the Russian and Chinese Revolutions. Hitler, who had initially joined the Nazi party as its propagandist, was quite familiar with the psychology of mobs and crowds.[83] Much of what he wrote about propaganda merely echoes the ideas of Gustave Le Bon, who had laid down principles of crowd psychology in the nineteenth century when he described the existence of the collective mind, which was primitive, excitable, sentimental, effeminate (meaning illogically emotional) and prone to destruction. Hitler perhaps had even greater contempt for the masses than did Le Bon.

Crowds and masses are also prone to *visionary rumors* — e.g., the Lady of Fatima in Portugal who appeared to crowds of spectators in relatively modern times. In the early 1960s, psychologist Carl Jung analyzed the Unidentified Flying Object craze as just the sort of mass visionary rumor that may appear in times when the collective unconsciousness was troubled — in these cases by the war and the Atomic Age. Hitler himself, viewed from this distance, seems possibly to have existed in the mass German consciousness as a sort of visionary rumor. I am not so sure about Ronald Reagan or Barack Obama, but if one

---

83 See again, Le Bon's *The Crowd*, which remains both an influential and highly readable work.

compares the public phenomena to the actual men (if one can abstract this far), they seem more mass visionary images than actual men.

If one watches Nazi propaganda films such as *Triumph of the Will*, the role of mass spectacles and groups in creating the mass mind and social reality of Nazi Germany becomes apparent. When the messianic Hitler arrives by airplane in Nuremberg, the shadow of his plane, the presence of the great one, passes over marching formations, organized crowds, in the streets. What an image! Crowd and group organization are key to everything. Virtually every scene of *Triumph of the Will* features elaborately staged events involving large, well-organized groups of people. They are beheld in perfectly laid out tent cities, often dressed alike in uniform, in formation, or even in supposedly playful moments, e.g., hundreds of clean young men cavorting, blanket-tossing one another and grooming *en masse* before enjoying their communal breakfast. The Nazi Party had something in the way of a group experience for virtually everyone, e.g., the Hitler youth organization. Individual consciousness became a teaspoon in an ocean of mass consciousness. And forget not that the Nazi party was an *Arbeiterpartei* — a worker's party — thus evoking the power of another powerful group identity, a set of norms, beliefs composing the Old World Germanic work ethic. The Nazi boy scout-like gatherings depicted in *Triumph of the Will* were obviously calculated to build and reinforce a certain civic collective character required for public works. We must not forget that the Nazis were socialists, which is itself a collectivist group mind-state that demands conformity in thought and deed, the so-called *ideology* and *praxis* associated with Marxism.[84]

Another aspect of modern horizontal propaganda is intolerance toward unaligned or preexisting groups, or natural organic groups or other groups that existed before the introduction of a new horizontal propaganda. Corporately created, modern horizontal propaganda is also inimical to any new, autonomous groups that may form outside or despite its influence. Corporate administrators appear instinctually to hate unions.

Freedom of association of groups was regarded as so powerful and basic in democratic social action that it is guaranteed by the American First Amendment. Totalitarians cannot brook freedom of association.

---

84 The socialistic aspect of the Nazis is a fact that modern socialists/collectivists seem to dislike revisiting.

Therefore, for example, the emerging corporate university does not well tolerate the traditional departmental disciplinary structure of universities, with self-governance, faculty senates and elected department chairs, because such structures are far too autonomous, resilient, and successfully resistant to the excesses of managerial fancy.

In order for horizontal propaganda to work effectively, subjects must to some fairly large extent give themselves over to the new group structure, either by peer pressure, force or through incentives. By definition, one cannot belong or owe allegiance to numerous primary groups — i.e., groups upon which an individual depends for survival — otherwise they would not be "primary." Also for this reason people having strong preexisting cultural or group ties may be generally immune to newly introduced horizontal propaganda as well as to vertical propaganda. Members of such autonomous groups do not easily succumb because such groups by their nature maintain their own preferred interpretations of the meaning of reality. They do not need someone else to do this for them, and often will resist intrusive attempts by explaining them away, dismissing them as nonsense, simply ignoring them or by fighting back, informationally or physically. Preexisting groups thus must be broken, bypassed or destroyed. Of course, groups without significant political or social agendas can usually be safely overlooked. The breaking up of extant groups is sometimes called reorganizing or reengineering the organization.

In the Korean War, attempts at "brainwashing" by the communist Chinese hinged upon the managed disruption of the normal group structures and hierarchy of American soldiers who had been taken as prisoners of war. Officers and enlisted men were assigned arbitrarily to new groups where an enlisted man or draftee might now be the leader. Interminable group discussions facilitated by Chinese political officers wore down resistance, a process that was augmented by poor food, isolation from home, lack of objective news about the world and loss of traditional social supports and structures.

In a sense, though, the Chinese were only doing to the Americans what they had been doing to themselves in the course of their own Communist revolution over the previous few years — breaking up traditional group structures and placing everyone into small groups where they became subject to intense coordinate pressures (and information control). This is what "radical" reforms entail. Such societies also breed collaborators and informants.

A particularly vicious tactic used by Chairman Mao Tse-tung was to encourage free democratic discussion in the form of group criticism to improve the system, during an era known as the Hundred Flowers movement in 1956-57. Authorities later imprisoned or killed those whose tongues had been loosened by the constructive group atmosphere and had provided "constructive criticism." There is no such thing as constructive criticism under many regimes, unless regime leaders are doing it themselves as a show of conspicuous virtue. As can be imagined, Hundred Flowers survivors were those people who guarded their opinions. For another totalitarian treatment involving groups, while implementing the Russian Revolution, Stalin found that the Kulak peasant farmers, who possessed strong group culture/identity and therefore were largely immune to collectivist propaganda, had to be reorganized out of existence. He killed or starved millions of them as a matter of policy.

Rigged Committees and Pseudo-Democracy

In the modern Western corporation or organizational environment the ad hoc task force or special committee becomes a forum to demonstrate conformity and in which to isolate deviance. Corporate walls do indeed have ears, a system abetted by gossip networks and corporate climbers currying favor. Additionally, it is very easy for employers and administrators to set up groups that give the appearance of democracy and participation, that are in reality everything but. A task force chaired by hand-selected "co-conveners" and participants has a destination preordained by whoever has done the pre-selection. For example, colleagues of mine who took part in extensive "roundtable" discussions concerning the strategic directions of their college reported that their numerous comments and ideas were not to be found in the final report, where only the ideas of the select group appointed by administrators appeared. As with the crowd agitators mentioned above, a small number of such "plants" can predetermine the trajectory of a group, especially when most participants are naïvely well-meaning. Such groups produce not only the appearance of democracy — of faculty governance in this instance — but also have other effects useful to administrators. As with Kurt Lewin's organ meats experiment, people who are included will often buy into the idea, or "take ownership" in today's corporate-speak. They rationalize their participation by saying and appearing to believe things such as "Well, some good ideas came out of it." Also, the select committee tactic allows administrators the strong defense of later saying, if criticized, that this was all "your idea," that faculty or employees, or whomever the manipulated ones may be, have "signed off on the program," "bought in," or had their "chance to contribute." We believe in "shared governance," they say, but their view of it is administrators doling out the shares and the work, maintaining the credit and the money, but never the blame. It's really more like "shared management."[85] It may be very difficult for critics to overcome these sorts of defenses because people outside the process may be naïve concerning the difference between an administratively created group and an autonomous group that sets it own agendas and picks it own leadership. This may be a too subtle point to differentiate for someone who has only a superficial knowledge of events and even less interest. This is also a reason why administrators (who also control the flow of information) can so consistently get away with this sort of nonsense. Also, administrators themselves often do not understand the differences between group types, or may be possessed by an in-group bias that makes them feel morally unimpeachable. They may quite honestly claim good intentions.

Commissions, councils, boards and committees generally are much manipulated in the modern organizational environment so as to smooth out wrinkles, e.g. the contention, discussion and unmanageability of true democracy. A managerial science exists in the so-called human services organizations where professional "staff" often lead board and committee chairs by the nose.[86] Even though the staff person ostensibly functions to facilitate the chair and other officers — the staff person being seen but not heard in public meetings — the main role of the staff person is often to feed ideas, materials, agendas and so forth to the officers, who then step forward in public to reap the recognition

---

85 My highly esteemed colleague, Professor David Nemeth made this remark over lunch.

86 John Tropman has written insightfully on the management of committees in human service organizations. His approach is much more benign and positive than my limited description here of abuses of committees. Tropman aims at maximizing the quality of decisions made by groups, an approach I admire and which works well among equals, but which presupposes benign intentions that are often not present in organizational environments. See *Committee Management in Human Services* (Chicago: Nelson-Hall, 1992).

that feeds their egos and fattens their careers. This is considered a good symbiotic tradeoff because both staff and board members benefit. Decisions tend to be fixed beforehand, including the pre-selection of chairs and officers, and then legitimized by the appearance of democratic process and input. Power lies in the right to nominate, designate and control agendas. Plus, because true democracy—a messier and more contentious affair in outward appearance—often does not make for good press, such inside practices provide good information control as well.

Shills and Judas Goats

Social pressure can be applied by simulating group situations to trap the unwary. A shill is a person who is employed by "the house" in gambling establishments to pretend to gamble. The "mark," the old carnival term for the fool about to be relieved of his money by some crooked game of chance, sees other people gambling and having fun, and even winning (it's all house money being exchanged at this point) and is thus encouraged to play. This works all the better if shills are sexually attractive. Restaurants and other merchandising establishment may use shills as well. A crowd attracts.

The Judas Goat inhabits slaughterhouses where sheep are killed. When the sheep arrive by truck they are often unwilling to go down the ramp to the kill floor—they smell blood, no doubt, and otherwise sense the great wrongness of the situation. The Judas Goat is introduced to lead the sheep down the ramp. The sheep, being social animals accustomed to a social order, follow their fellow quadruped down the ramp. Once arriving at the kill floor, the Judas Goat is led away and rewarded for his work. The sheep do not fare as well. I need not point out that humans are social animals as well.

Ersatz, Vicarious and Virtual Groups

As Harold Lasswell noted, elites invariably speak for the common good. In politics, it is usual to claim to speak for the people, various publics, or large groups of people, e.g., interest groups, the masses, the American people or various oppressed subclasses. This so-called "public opinion" then is used as a normative force or standard that can be brought to bear on various issues. Mass media news often represents polling or surveys as a sort of reality tester — the Ultimate-Interpretational-Church-of-What's- Happening-Now: 47 percent want Jones; 47 Smith, while the remainder is undecided or doesn't care. In any case, hearing polls and participating in polls seems to be a way for the individual to connect to the group or to the herd. People seem to need cues on the correct direction, the trend, the meaning of modern times. No one wants to be a fossil. Polls, as such, appeal to some sort of deep herd alignment instinct.

Accordingly propagandists use them shamelessly — which is partly why all the major political parties have pollsters and conduct focus groups constantly to measure changing currents and depths and design effective appeals suitable to the moment. Surveys indicate directions to the herd, with various surveys for various herds conducted by various herders. If there is no evident "public opinion," it becomes necessary to create it through polls and so forth. One can do this merely by asking a question about, let's say, Haiti: "How do you feel about giving human aid to Haiti? Strongly disagree, disagree, neutral, agree or strongly agree?" The result is public opinion, by some definitions, even though respondents had no opinion of any sort on this matter before the question. One easily can design questions with which most people will agree or disagree, depending on the results desired.

Television programs often create an idealized (or simplified) ersatz group situation into which the audience member can project himself — thus providing an emotionally satisfying vicarious group experience, with coordinate social pressure, without the trouble of having to go anywhere or do anything like the real work of joining a group. As a passive conditioning system, this seems very effective over time.

When Joseph Goebbels, the Nazi propaganda minister, encountered television in the 1930s, then in its experimental state, he perceived it as the perfect group indoctrination "educational" medium. He envisioned groups of people watching together, as it then seemed too extravagantly expensive for individuals or even single families. Nowadays this economic miracle has come to pass — and so much the better for the propagandas of socialization delivered by the medium.

You have certainly noticed that many popular television entertainment shows are set up as a vicarious group experience. Popular shows of the 1950s-1970s, e.g., *Ozzie and Harriet* and *Leave it to Beaver*, were idealized families that imparted crude moral lessons on the values of honesty, hard work, etc. The lessons changed over time, diversity themes, for example, have replaced the Caucasian family patriarch, but the lessons are still just as ham-handedly delivered, underscored by the same old laugh tracks. Even the laugh track is a social cue, a means of exerting group pressure. The viewer follows the group norm and thoughtlessly laughs along. For example, *Roseanne*, with its working class packaging, allowed audience members to laughingly participate in the slow moral improvements of the show's characters, who became more accepting of diversity each and every episode. Many popular shows have been centered on the (mis)adventures of social groups sharing apartments, bars and coffee houses, and recently, allegedly deserted islands,[87] e.g., *Friends* and *Seinfeld*. All provide behavior models, character types, group norms and moral and psychological orientation. Today's so-called "reality shows" employ peer groups that fascinate the basest of instincts; the morality play appears perhaps too cerebral for this new genre, the main thrust seemingly a sort of behavioral hog wallow of egoism, consumerism, vanity and power — all of which can be very profitable for mass marketers. People seem to lose themselves in the vicarious group experience of these shows.

The online virtual group is coming on strongly and shows even more promise to change behavior and attitude because participation is both more select (thus indicating audience predispositions) and less passive. Facebook groups and online discussion forums allow disparate people to share sympathies and align; thusovercoming separation in time and space to some degree. Politics is increasingly informed by these online communities, many of which have become extremely effective in electoral politics. Marketers for products, news and entertainment routinely set up these online communities in which their consumer bases can meet, bleat, vote for plot lines, gossip about characters and develop and reinforce the belief systems and behavior that make these formats so useful to social managers.

As has been emphasized, horizontal propaganda induces behavior change. Propaganda researchers in America learned this back in the Second World War era when conducting funded research for the government. The fields of social psychology and much modern management theory taught in business schools owe their existence to

---

87 *Gilligan's Island* in this regard is not all that much different from *Lost*.

the administrative search for group-management techniques. Indeed, today more social psychology is taught in management classes, albeit watered down, than in university psychology departments. Communist/socialist regimes of the twentieth century routinely used horizontal propaganda to institutionalize their revolutions. Businesses use it to attempt to get more out of employees. In such applications individuals are placed in committees or political study groups. In businesses team management horizontal propaganda binds employees in a multidimensional, ever-changing net of expectations and normative pressures toward conformity.

A social action paradox at work here is that true democracy is perhaps only possible among small groups, where everyone is equal and can discuss and participate, while at the same time the use of group pressure to suffocate democracy and independent action is perhaps the greatest threat of our time. Modern administrative science has thoroughly compromised the autonomy of groups.

The Fifth Commandment

COGNITIVELY PENETRATE
AND STICK

The propagandist must somehow make a cognitive impression in a perceptually cluttered society, where ceaseless yammering from multiple sources is the norm: cell phones, televisions, text messaging, meetings, radio, iPods, pagers, emails, 24 hour news broadcasts, the various burgeoning social media, infotainment, fliers, billboards — a world where even breakfast cereal boxes demand attention. Quietude seems a contemporary abomination. Every moment distracts. Rather than a "disorder," attention deficit seems the contemporary order of things. So how does one get attention?

Cognitive penetration was probably relatively easier in the far past, or in the early days of mass society when people had literally just come off the farm and phenomena such as bright neon lights and the barker at the strip club or carnival sideshow were still considered novelties. These old standards are often still reliable due to unchanging human needs. Sex still sells, for example, and probably always will. A good-looking woman generally outsells or interpersonally out-communicates

her plain sister when it comes to message reception; nobody wants
to hire an ugly waitress. But when the perceptual world is filled with
pneumatic women beyond count, as on television, where hundreds of
channels bark instead of just three or so as it was in the early days
of broadcasting, when legions of sources compete for attention 24/7,
what then? As always, pragmatic considerations guide propaganda,
which is why propaganda should be considered both art and science,
or more precisely, a scientifically informed art.[88] Propagandists do
what demonstrably works — theory lags behind — and are ever alert
for promising, new methods.

To make the message penetrating and memorable, the propagandist may make use of many techniques, not all at once of course, but
often in combination. An exhaustive listing is impossible. I can provide an overview of chief techniques, while noting they are practiced
in many variations. Just to be clear, *cognitive penetration* is achieved
when a message is both noticed and retained at some mental level,
for the unnoticed is just noise while the unretained may as well have
never been.

Some of the chief means of cognitive penetration are: *novelty,*
which includes humor; *repetition and simplicity* such as slogans, strik-
ing symbols, graphics and images, often delivered by sheer vulgar
shouting or its visual equivalent as in a "loud" necktie; so-called *lexical
means* such as metaphor, schema, acronyms, alliteration, rhyme, word
choice and style; *salience/interest,* which includes basic needs like food,
sex, economic survival and direct personal involvement; and by what
I call *gnostic* techniques aimed at producing the appearance of hidden underground knowledge, censorship, or controversy all of which
possess the allure of the forbidden. Few of these techniques have clear
boundaries separating one from the other. Although ancient, most
have been streamlined and amplified by modern media technology.[89]
All work some of the time, none work all of the time, most work often,

---

88 Jacques Ellul advanced this opinion.

89 The old joke about mule training applies here — a mule being much like the target
audience of the propagandist. A man attempting to train his mule became frustrated,
picked up a board and begin hitting the mule over the head with it. Whereupon a
second man, observing, said, "Wait, that's not the way to do it. I am a professional
mule trainer and I will show you how." The second man then picks up the board and
gives the mule a whopping blow over the head. The first man asks, "Why did you do
that? I thought you said that wasn't the way." Said the second man, "Well, first you
have to get his attention."

and all are more or less dependent on the nature of the intended audience and the situation. Entire books on persuasion and propaganda go no deeper than elaborating on these sorts of techniques in the form of sales and advertising tricks.[90] They comprise the outward surface of propaganda that people may often notice. This assumes that anything is noticed at all, for mostly these techniques depend for their effectiveness on uncritical, mindless absorption. But because mindfulness requires energy, which is a limited resource, we are all vulnerable at least some of the time.

Novelty

Boredom, staleness, ennui exist as facts of life. They cumulatively kill the spirit, especially when satisfaction from other sources is lacking, e.g., being trapped in a meaningless job, or the experience of going nowhere fast. People seek new experiences that taste of something unknown, such as the promise of greater fulfillment, a road to happiness, a new sex partner, the orgasmic hamburger, the unique thrill, the rare possession, and so on.

Thus motivated, people are by nature suckers for the "new and improved," some more than others, of course. Even longtime standard product brands must regularly announce changes and improvements, albeit no more than an updated container, a new miracle ingredient, or use of up-to-date buzzwords (a term which has itself become a *buzzword*) such as *sustainability, green, eco-friendly* and *recycled,* all of which will soon go stale as well. In business and organizational propaganda, words and phrases appear such as "transformational change," and seem to mean no more than "new and improved."

Novelty includes the grotesque as well as the super-beautiful and the exotic. "News," a saleable product much like any other product, by definition is that which is new or novel. New beginnings also attract, such as being reborn or saved. Some churches offer classes on the mysterious (to me, at least) process of re-virginization, a renewal that involves signing a pledge and I cannot imagine what else. New

---

90 Do not overlook that from a propaganda perspective there is little difference between selling a politician and a brand of soap, an observation based on CPI director George Creel's comment about how he sold the First World War to the American public.

automobile models call out to those who must have the latest develop-ment. The need for novelty may be satisfied by revolution, renaissance, progress, technological marvels, octuplets, the newest pop music sensation, independent suspension and whomever the next new star-let or celebrity sensation is or is not sleeping with at any particular moment. The gory and perversely weird all have their season. So does the wholesome.

Even novelty gets old, however. So the pitchman changes up with something different and comparatively novel — good "old-fashioned" quality or values. But very little is truly novel, and most people would probably not be able to apprehend something that is, for as the Second Commandment of propaganda advises: propaganda must reflect the values and beliefs of the audience at the risk of not being understood at all. The idea or appearance of novelty works well, however, as does a spurious or superficial sort of novelty that is not too disturbing to the equilibrium of audience members. We could refer to this as "conven-tional" novelty.

Examples mentioned so far have been relatively innocuous and superficial — and if a person persists in foolishness throughout life there is no help for it, anyway. Where novelty does apparently seri-ous damage is at the political and administrative levels of society. Here I speak of *The Program*. The Program is modern administrative cul-ture's new and improved product, the justification for the existence of administrative elites. By means of programs and proposals they dem-onstrate leadership capabilities, efficiency and their value to society. Programs purportedly solve social or business problems, some as old as Man, others inherent to modern mass society. What administrators do via programs, allegedly, is to creatively marshal scarce resources (resources always being limited) to solve the chief problems faced by the organization or society. What administrators do in reality is to recycle old platitudes and ideas, giving them trendy new names. Thus, they briefly shine. A typical example is from the field of education. Educational administrators must, let's say, deal with the problem of teaching mathematics and reading to children, a tedious but essential business that is much easier to talk about than to do, which is precisely why it is not done. So they announce a new program that will use technology to teach children. Instead of a blackboard, wax tablet and stylus, book or workbook (all technologies that have worked as well as any) and a teacher who demands attention, now the child is imagined miraculously absorbing the same information from a computer screen, assured of receiving even less attention than before. It sounds good to parents who have consigned the vital education of their children to officialdom's high-sounding promises rather than to take personal responsibility that entails tedious work. The Board of Education of the City of Detroit, for example, has a warehouse full of expensive, allegedly pedagogically advanced, reading programs purchased with taxpayer money. Millions. The miracle cure doesn't help however, because no magic technology imparts reading, math or writing. You cannot just "hook them up to a computer," as I once heard it put. Work, time, individual attention and commitment are required — all things in short supply. After a season, the program tarnishes. Interest recedes — and the next program for whatever trend happens to be looming is rolled in, and the basic problem remains the basic problem. More room must then be found in the warehouse.

Via its programs, administration traffics in hope rather than results. Any program may give two or three years of resume-building trumpeting, however. Since administrators can usually largely control the flow of information concerning their organizations, recalling the First Commandment, administrators can often sustain themselves for considerable periods of time by carefully contrived evaluations and measurements of the program's alleged effects.[91] Functionally equivalent to carpetbaggers in many ways, administrators are likely to move on before the total collapse of their house of cards.[92] Or they announce a new program to address a new crisis. The old one is silted over by the sands of bureaucratic forgetfulness.

The Program is change not only for the sake of change, i.e., novelty, but for personal enrichment and self-justification, the program being the *modus operandi* of modern executive culture. If things happen to go right, be assured that the propagandist will claim his program is responsible. If wrong, then a new program is needed, giving administrators even more thematic material with which to work and a new story to peddle. Programs also have the comforting effect of creating the illusion of understanding and responding to the problem, thus reducing general anxiety arising from fear of chaos.

---

91 See again Altheide and Johnson's *Bureaucratic Propaganda.*
92 See Robert Jackall's, *Moral Mazes: The World of Corporate Managers* (New York: Oxford University Press, 2010).

Humor

Humor offers another path to cognition. It is related to novelty — for humor generally revolves around incongruity, a novel, unexpected, if not outright bizarre way of looking at something. The irrational or post-modern types of appeals that seem to capture the attention of youthful markets appear to also function via a jarring sort of novelty. When a person has been raised as a media baby — television being probably the number one babysitter in the Western world — virtually everything becomes commonplace. Therefore, a way to get noticed is by offering something jarring, quirky and impossible — e.g., a recent anti-perspiration ad where a young man sprays water from his armpits. Being noticed usually trumps either good taste or reason. Effective propaganda need not be rational, but it cannot go unnoticed.

Repetition and Simplicity

Propagandists have long recognized repetition and simplicity as twin tracks on which mass propaganda rides. Keep it simple and repeat it often. This maxim is the basis of modern mass media advertising. Hitler extolled the principle, too, because he thought the masses were intellectually dull. The basic notion here is that people may be less than bright (especially *en masse*), busy, distracted, involved in their own affairs or those of others, uncaring, illiterate, daydreaming or uncomprehending. Attention span and available personal energy also limit cognition. Add to this mix ubiquitous media over-stimulation that competes for whatever leftover attention may be potentially available in any one person or group. A complicated message, therefore, stands little chance of reaching its target intact. This is the reason why so much advertising sounds as if it were designed for the needs of those who ride to school on "the special bus." Even supposedly sophisticated audiences are quite limited in this regard, more so than individuals comprising the audience may imagine. Cognitive simplicity also links with the need for propaganda to disambiguate, recalling the Third Commandment.

Simplicity and repetition explain the frequent usefulness of slogans, for example, "Change you can believe in," which if one repeats often enough sounds like it may even mean something tangible. Notice the ambiguity of the words, though. It is paradoxical that something so absolutely ambiguous can provide an illusion of simplicity. Does this slogan mean "real" change or just a promised change that will fool you into belief? Nakedly considered, it seemingly means not much of anything at all, except as a vaguely motivating idea that can be pounded into people's heads through multimedia repetition via bumper stickers, chants, posters, lapel pins, duplicated and multiplied through news broadcasts and commercials. This simplified message is merely an arbitrary sign selected for its ease of insertion and retention. Conditioning through repetition does the rest. This conditioning builds an associational link with the source (the Obama-Biden 2008 presidential campaign, in this instance). Its vagueness also allows people to project into the slogan whatever meaning they most need to see: at the personal level it may take on very specific meanings. Slogans have proved their worth many times over, e.g., "Shovel-ready projects," where the slogan had much more substance than the projects.

Simplicity and repetition amount to pure behavioral conditioning. See it, hear it, associate it with the source and repeat until imprinted. The audience member becomes the behavioral psychologist's rat. There are good reasons behind exposure to the same commercial twenty times or more in the same evening. It takes that long to get through.

There have been thousands of such slogans and catch phrases, many far more clever and poignant than the one cited above. They are associated with movements, political campaigns, issue and commercial advertising. Here are just a few: *Ein Volk, ein Reich, ein Führer*; Tippecanoe and Tyler, too; Geico — 15 minutes could save you 15 percent or more on car insurance; Have it Your Way; Hell No, We Won't Go; Take Back America; Chew Mail Pouch; Just Say No. The list expands all the time. You can probably find dozens in the junk piles of your memory.[93]

Through simplicity and repetition, an association can be also forged between an organized cause and a symbol, corporate logo, jingle or character — be it cartoon character, an actor or otherwise.

---

93 But how many can recite the Declaration of Independence or any substantial portions of the Bill of Rights? Think about the meaning of that. Regarding slogans, a personal favorite is, "When Adam delved and Eve span, who was then the gentleman?" a pornographically ambiguous rhyming slogan associated with English peasant revolts in medieval times. I cannot provide a source.

Consider here the cute little talking gecko with the indeterminate British Commonwealth accent, until recently merely a lizard, but now so much more because of the forging by simplicity and repetition. Consider the swastika, which before Hitler was merely a fairly common architectural motif and mystical symbol, but now forever linked to dark Nazism. The donkey and the elephant represent philosophies of America's major political parties. The Mercedes Benz logo reigns as a sign of luxurious quality. Corporate and university logos forge similar associations, "branding" in marketing-speak, e.g., the University of Michigan logo.

Keep it simple. Repeat frequently. Keep pounding.

Lexical Techniques

The term *lexical* refers to choice of words or style, such as technical, folkish, or authoritarian language, big words versus small words, jargon, diction and other techniques common to speechmaking and persuasion via spoken or written words. When people refer to *rhetoric* they often mean these lexical aspects of public communication.

All sorts of lexical techniques, also known as *rhetorical devices*, have been cataloged over the centuries. An Internet search on "rhetorical devices" will reveal dozens, some quite obscure, some quite subtle. Many are very powerful at achieving cognitive penetration if used judiciously, because they make language memorable, dramatic and visualizable. Again, such effects are audience-dependent. Using them once or twice achieves novelty, overuse equates with droning ponderousness, the inflated style of the old-time politician. Here I will merely mention and give examples of some of the more common techniques/devices such as metaphor, acronyms, alliteration, rhyme, word choice/style and asyndeta.

Metaphors and similes are useful because they promote both quick understanding and recollection. Even though this understanding may be false or incomplete, as with any analogy, it can still serve the purposes of the propagandist. Do not overlook that merely understanding some concept is halfway to persuasion, if not more, and a metaphor, if grasped, creates a sudden understanding that aids in alignment with the desired way of thinking.

An example from the past is the metaphor of America as a "melting pot." This assimilation propaganda arose in the days of massive European immigration. Irish, Poles, Germans, Central Europeans, Italians, Greeks all arrived on American shores, shed their national identities, and became over time Americans who spoke one language (English) in one nation, under God, with liberty, etc. This crucible metaphor (recall the Crucible of Democracy) in which elemental substances combine to form a uniform, useful and strong metallic alloy, was generally understandable to the worker ants of the industrial revolution. A current diversity-assimilation theme metaphor is the rainbow, which can be understood[94] with but slight explanation and little or no English.

Corporate officers and business conservatives have been prone to metaphors such as "Trickle-down Economics" or the "Business Model" which suggest that letting businesspeople have their way produces benefits that will trickle down to the lower classes, creating jobs and prosperity for the little people too (although one can't use the term "little people" anymore, now that almost everyone thinks they are middle class). Even universities are now subjected to the business model metaphor, which means lower production costs, standardization and chintzy, feel-good branding. Terms like *depression* and *recession* or *slump* are essentially metaphors used as cognitive shorthand for a bewildering set of poorly understood factors that affect the general economy. Corporate and political propagandists often use them to evade blame or take credit (via programs). Detroit was first "The Motor City" and then, soon after, "The Renaissance City," suggesting vitality and discouraging the uncomfortably popular epithet "The Murder City." Other powerful metaphors include the Contract with America, the Cold War, the Iron Curtain, the Social Safety Net, the War on Drugs, the Academic Journey and No Child Left Behind. Recollect also President Ronald Reagan's much-circulated speech at the Berlin Wall, "Mr. Gorbachev, tear down this wall," intended literally, but especially metaphorically. That whole speech consisted of little more than repetition and simplicity employed to deliver a vivid

---

94 We should consider that functionally — the idea of "diversity" in many organizations, especially universities and government, provides a morally unimpeachable base for administrators and administrative programs, allowing them to justify their existence with an absolutist moral philosophy. How can one even think about criticizing diversity these days?

metaphor. A last example, the much-vaunted *information superhighway* seems to be turning out to be more of a toll road.

Acronyms, if used judiciously, also tend to lodge in memory. How many of the following rather specialized terms do you recognize? IED, IUD LASER, IRS, SOSAD, NRA/ILA, ACLU, AARP, AFL/CIO, FBI, CIA, USA, RPG, INRI, NAZI, HIV/AIDS, ADD, STD, SDS, HUD. Acronyms function as effective mnemonics, meaning that lasting cognitive penetration has been achieved. An exception is when they are used excessively, as when military personnel use them to attempt conversation with non-military persons. Acronyms, however, are also used to signify expert knowledge, real or pretend, and hence are part of virtually any modern technical jargon. Because acronyms may convey expert status, and may condense a program to a memorable byte, they well serve propagandistic purposes. Social service, educational and corporate programs use acronyms often, especially the type that I call the *summary acronym*, which works by forming easily remembered action words, e.g., LEAD = Leadership Education and Development, SOSAD = Save our Sons and Daughters, or DARE, which you have already encountered above.[95]

Propagandistic penetration can also be produced via *alliteration*, the repeated use of words beginning with the same consonant sound, e.g., the phrase, "judged not by the color of their complexion but by the content of their character," which appears to have been delivered in variations on more than one occasion by M. L. King. That indeed the technique enhances penetration is shown by the fact that you probably recognized the speaker immediately. Alliterative, rather than rhymed, poetry was the general mode in Northern Europe in the oral tradition. Before literacy became common, works such as Beowulf were recited and passed down precisely because alliteration made them memorizeable — e.g., "the hero unlocked his word horde." Or from modern advertising for women's hair care products, "Super. Smooth. Silky." Modern corporate alliteration often tends more toward the banal — e.g., the Power of a Penny Program or Campus Crusade for Christ. Much corporate stuff is so horribly banal that it needs to be dressed up in this fashion to pass for something interesting.

---

95 While working on this book, I attempted to produce a summary acronym that would serve as a mnemonic for the Ten Commandments, based on the word PROPAGAN-DAS or COMMANDMENT. Obviously, I failed.

Rhyme is obvious enough and effective in measured doses. Rhymes grease recall. Jingles and ditties from commercials infect the modern consciousness. Eighty-year olds still remember the Burma Shave road signs spaced out along highways in the pre-interstate highway era, delivering poetic messages, a line every hundred yards, on the tangible social benefits of the product:

Doesn't
Kiss you
Like she useter?
Perhaps she's seen
A smoother rooster!

Word choice also affects penetration. In general, since Aristotle prescribed rhetorical techniques, the recognized best general course is to use plain everyday language that employs the usual meaning of words in the everyday sense. One does not sprinkle a message with French or Latin literary terms at the local town hall meeting. One is also role-consistent. A middle-aged white male managerial type does not speak in what he thinks is Ebonics, hoping to improve cognitive penetration with a youthful black audience, unless he is looking for comic effect or to be treated like a buffoon. As an academic, I am expected to be a little fancy, but must reign in my language so that the eyes in general audiences won't glaze over — this is true when speaking to students as well. As always, keep it simple and consider the audience. Exceptions exist. Don't obviously talk down to an audience, as this insults. Some audiences may demand a degree of puffery in language — e.g., academics and business people who regard themselves as elite. Poetic, high-blown word choice is especially appropriate on ceremonial or celebratory occasions, where one can speak of "Death's Dark Door" and such without fear of offending, baffling or violating expectations, for there are certain ritualistic aspects of such events and certain things that need to be said in certain ways to assure all present that the cosmic order still reigns. Also, American presidential and political rhetoric has become more and more ceremonial over time, and the president has become more of a celebrant than an executive, e.g., *the shining city on a hill*, etc. But in everyday propaganda, especially to mass audiences, straightforward and simple usually works best.

Asyndeta are used mainly for dramatic closings or transitions. I mention this technique here just to give a taste of the sort of interesting devices that old-time rhetoricians bestowed on today's propaganda practices. An asyndeton is a short dramatic series of words or phrases, unconnected by conjunctions such as "and," "but" and "or": e.g., "I came. I saw. I conquered." They are useful in mass advertising and in corporate and political speeches. They may be used to close legal trials — "You know the facts. You see the evidence. You know the verdict. Guilty." They are also especially useful as "closers" in job interviews and sales because they provide a good in-your-face ending. I have myself used them successfully — e.g., "You know my experience. You know I have ability. I want the job." At which one person looked at me, blinked, and said, "Oh…OK." But don't overdo it. Once a technique calls attention to itself, its usefulness is compromised because audience members realize they are being worked. You probably noticed, for example, that I used an asyndeton to close the section above on repetition and simplicity: "Keep it simple. Repeat frequently. Keep pounding."

Salience/Interest

We are all solipsistic creatures to a high degree, as well as being much dependent on looking out for Number One. Propagandists design and direct messages accordingly.

Local interest stories attract attention precisely because they are local — one cannot get away with ignoring the immediate environment. And preexisting interests largely determine future interests. These are the main reasons for customized appeals to specific audiences, locales, conditions, hobbies, interests and so forth. Hemorrhoid sufferers pay attention when the subject of relief comes up. Modern marketing and political communications increasingly utilize digitalization and computer-generated lists that make it possible to correlate interests and individual behaviors. For example, it is no problem at all nowadays to generate a list of registered voters in a district who have also purchased hunting licenses. These people can then be approached directly with mass-customized political messages, fundraising appeals or sales solicitations that may suit them. Any list of people with a collective interest — magazine subscribers, sports fans, attendees at a political event, association members, rubber fetishists, etc. — functions as an avenue to penetration.

Gnostic Techniques

A last set of penetrators that will be discussed in this chapter can be loosely categorized into what I call *gnostic techniques* that produce an appearance of hidden underground knowledge, the lure of the forbidden, the appearance of controversy, of dark and therefore compelling conspiracy theories. Censorship or the simulation of censorship also produces roughly this same effect. In all cases, the "secret" knowledge, simply by having been designated as secret or forbidden, suddenly becomes much more desirable and interesting.

The term *gnostic* refers to knowledge, i.e., "to know." Gnosticism has proven itself over time as a very strong human impulse. A gnome was once believed to be an elusive dwarf-like creature that lived in the earth and knew many great secrets. Gnostic cults of various sorts have arisen repeatedly throughout history, organized around sacred mysteries and occult truths, some bizarrely arcane. Accordingly, many organizations thrive on secrecy and initiation rites. The Masons, for example, have secret knowledge that is shared with initiates when they reach the proper stage of development. That which is hidden or forbidden excites many people, who feel that the good stuff is not just laying around on the surface for all to see. It *must* be hidden. Even Biblical gospels and parables have been interpreted as gnostic tales with hidden meanings intended only for those who have ears to understand. To the Gnostic, this means himself, the one who is "in the know" while other people are oblivious to the truth, those poor schmucks.

Always-popular conspiracy theories reek of Gnosticism. The Nazis and others believed that the Jews sought world domination, a conspiracy theory maintaining that a secret cabal of Jews controlled mass media, commerce and international banking. Many people still believe this. Or the secret, mysterious cabal becomes the Masons, or the Left, or the Right — same dance, different tune. The more secret, esoteric and mysterious, the more alluring it is.

People *in the know* can spot and interpret the signs while the unenlightened behave like unknowing cattle doomed for slaughter. People love the mystery of it all. There are good pragmatic reasons why Sacred

Mysteries are so often part of religions.[96] Also, as is apparent, the gnostic theory flatters its believer, who by embracing it regards himself smarter than other people. Snob appeals in marketing operate in a similar fashion — the consumer who knows the secrets of the gourmet pasta or single malt liquor will pay much more for it, at least more than it is probably worth, and think himself smart in the bargain. A euphemistic phrase one sometimes hears about this practice is "the educated consumer," which as far as I can tell means having been educated to pay more for exotic stuff that is allegedly in relatively short supply, even though the people selling the stuff never seem to run out of what they are selling.

Regarding penetration through censorship and controversy, I truly hope that some organization will censor or try to ban this book, for it will likely increase its popularity. As mentioned previously, the Roman Catholic Church maintained an index of prohibited books until the 1960s. It abandoned the practice when it was finally realized that placing a book on the index caused it to sell more. James Joyce's *Ulysses* became a best-selling artsy novel, I believe, because U.S. Customs once banned its import into America. The media attention it received in this way was the best marketing campaign possible (and came at no cost to the publisher). It is difficult to believe that most people who eventually bought *Ulysses*, or received it as a book of the month club selection, could possibly have appreciated Joyce's esoteric lexical-sexual acrobatics. They bought it because it had been forbidden. I also doubt that most people can even understand the relatively few "dirty parts," as they are so overlain with Joyce's artful literary allusions as to be generally obscure. But because it had indeed been banned, it therefore demanded looking at. Because of such unintended promotions some elites, who attempt to control the flow of information, have learned that it is usually a better strategy to ignore contrary information than to rise to the bait by denouncing it. If you like this book, please demand publicly that it be banned.

The 1960s and 1970s generations saw tremendous growth of what could be called the propaganda-of-controversy used as a marketing technique to a body of consumers that became known as the counterculture. Let me illustrate by an example: the entertainer Bob Dylan.

---

96 Hannah Arendt said that people believe in conspiracy theories precisely because of this general mysteriousness.

Notice it wasn't "Robert Dylan" or Zimmerman, his real name, but just
"Bob." He was a romanticized creature who sang obscure lyrics, e.g.,
"The sun ain't yellow its chicken," into which people read deep meanings. He was a rebel who sang about life on the street. He even taught
the Beatles to smoke marijuana, so it was said, he was that outrageously
cool, a revolutionary. He rode a motorcycle, about which there were
dark rumors of a serious accident, all very underground, but a major
transnational media corporation sold his recordings. Dylan is really
about as revolutionary as General Motors. The image was the product.
It was great marketing that sold almost a whole generation of "rebels."
It reminds also of the various blues sensations that recording compa-
nies promoted into consciousness, all with names like "Blind Willey
Dog Jefferson" as proof of their underground authenticity.

Consider, too, recent rap and hip hop artists — whose cop killer lyrics, sexual obscenities and misogyny have caused apparent outrage.
But their recordings are also highly commercial products of major corporations. You are getting the idea. Nowadays such marketing is fairly
routine — the canned revolution. Controversy is easy to manufacture.
P.T. Barnum, the man who allegedly coined the expressions, "Without
promotion something terrible happens — nothing," used to denounce
himself before his traveling show arrived in a new town. He would
send letters to the local newspapers under assumed names claiming
that he, P.T. Barnum, was a fraud. Then he would write under his own
name to defend himself from the charges. Modern entertainment and
literary news is still much the same sort of thing. Such controversy
penetrates and, better yet, often sells. Chances are that nowadays when
a movie, book, film or celebrity is denounced or talked about as con-
troversial, it is merely the marketing department doing their job.

Cognitively penetrate and stick in their craw.[97]

---

97 Even a bad, irritating ad or appeal can penetrate — which is better than not being
noticed. You notice also that television ads are delivered at an irritatingly higher
volume than content programming, which is only sensible because the advertisers are
paying the bills, and from the advertiser's perspective the advertisement is the only
content that matters.

The Sixth Commandment

DISTANCE THE PROPAGANDA
FROM ITS SOURCE

Propagandists often use front organizations and other means to distance themselves from their propaganda, thereby gaining the credibility (or the benefit of the doubt) inherent to "disinterested" third-party, scientific or objective information. [98]

They do this because message acceptance depends much on the known or imagined motives of the source. Any organization trying to "sell" an idea or product, which is what organizations must constantly do, is motivationally suspect. It is understood that in one way or another the source will benefit and we will pay. It's the same with politicians, administrators and social programs, all of which seek power by promising service and then extracting payment. Experience teaches distrust, for interested parties can be trusted mainly to look out for their own interests, whatever fair appearance they may assume and however they may dissemble. "Disinterested," supposedly objective

---

98 I am not at all sure what "objective" information is. All mass society information serves some purpose, and none of it spontaneously appears out of nothingness.

third parties, however, seem comparatively trustworthy. The propagandist disguises the propaganda accordingly.

For example, when the White House releases a report, without even having to bother to read it, most people know in advance that it will serve the interests of the President and his party. It doesn't much matter what the report says, what it's about, even if it is self-critical — for then it demonstrates honesty and forthrightness — the underlying purpose forwards organizational self-interest. We don't even need to read it to know this. This is because a main purpose of organizational communication is to take credit or dodge blame. Information is routinely — and quite sensibly — dismissed or ignored because of the obvious motives attributed to its source. But what happens when the same information is released independently by an unknown organization called — let's make one up — "Americans for Freedom?" How does one then regard the message and source? People are probably more likely to accept this information at face value, or at least give it a fair hearing, because it has no "history" or connotative "baggage," and not instantly dismiss it as they would if it was associated with the White House.

In my own system of thought, I call these distancing techniques *indirect means of propaganda*, although they really work by misdirection. Indirect techniques have been fundamental to mass propaganda for more than a century. There are a number of ways they are typically done.

A classic early example is the elevation of the banana from a comic curiosity, as in the song "Yes, I Have No Bananas!" to a dietary staple used as baby food. Edward Bernays credits himself with this accomplishment. Bernays appears to have invented the term "public relations," after working as a propagandist for the American government's Committee on Public Information in the First World War. He later applied wartime lessons to peacetime propaganda on behalf of various business and political interests. Bernay's client, the United Fruit Company, had access to a huge supply of bananas but was faced with the problem of insignificant market demand. So Bernays created a mass market via indirect means. He found an old report by an obscure physician on beneficial effects of bananas on infant digestion. He created a front organization with an innocuous sounding name, which distributed copies of the report and relayed this information to mass media outlets such as newspapers, women's magazines and any association that might be interested.

Bernays' technique worked. Bananas were elevated to the status of having been blessed by modern medical science and began to be sought as a healthful food, with United Fruit, of course, the unnamed beneficiary of a fad which became a habit. The same techniques are still regularly used to market health fads, dietary supplements and other, often questionable, products, like social programs. Indirect propaganda comes at you from unexpected angles disguised as news, talk shows, scientific reports, independent testing firms and other third-party information; and although the primary beneficiaries may be unnamed, they still benefit while you pay.

A recent example from politics, the so-called Swift Boat Veterans sprang up from seemingly nowhere to damage presidential candidate John Kerry's political reputation as a heroic Vietnam veteran. The organization later vanished just as quickly as it had appeared. Had the same information originated from the Bush campaign, it would have been dismissed as "politics." However, the veteran group appeared credible, and at least muddied the water, with the Bush-Cheney campaign the beneficiary.

Other typical indirect techniques include so-called "leaks" from government agencies, which may be planned attempts to influence public opinion; unnamed "reliable sources" mentioned in news articles; supposedly independent think tanks that are wholly financed by ideologues; ad hoc and citizens committees of various sorts that "spontaneously" appear to influence some issue and then disappear when the issue recedes from prominence. In the 1950s and 1960s, when the term "Communist" had even more negative connotations than it does now, there were many organizations of little substance that functioned as "Communist fronts," as they used to be called. Distributing supposedly subversive information, they produced what were then called "dupes."

Nowadays the term "astroturf" has been popularized to describe ghostly grass roots groups, although sometimes the term is used by detractors to dismiss the genuine efforts of real grass roots groups. I have myself witnessed obviously staged demonstrations by alleged "citizen committees" that appeared and disappeared as fast as the news cameras came and went, and were never seen or heard from again to my knowledge.

Non-profit organizations and various social service and political campaigns often have advisory boards of community leaders and notables that function, in effect, as a front organization. The notables merely lend their names and reputations to the effort. Any real steering, advising or information originates with organizational staff or principals in all such organizations of which I am aware, and the board is effectively nominal, serving for show purposes.

Consumers of information may find it impossibly difficult to establish the bona fides of such groups, committees, organizations or associations (whatever one chooses to call them). My undergraduate students tend to be frighteningly naïve about organizations. Except for a few very well-known associations with which they may be familiar, information from one group is pretty much as good as information from another for them. The tendency is to take such sources at face value.

Indirect information becomes even more untraceable once it has been filtered through news reports or other third-party media, as is generally the way these things go, thereby gaining even more credibility because it appears to have been vetted by independent, "critical" journalists. Such information laundering makes information seem clean when in fact it may be very dirty, e.g., "Reliable sources say..." or "An expert in the field reports..."

Reporters quite often use front organizations as news sources — and they too may have difficulties in sorting out the true nature of such groups. This is aggravated by the fact that these organizations in turn woo reporters, for functioning as a source for news and information is the primary mode of operation of these organizations, their very reason for existence. They make themselves convenient.

Let me give a specific example of how such information is sometimes reported in mass media news using the topic area of gun policy. Anyone at all politically attentive knows more or less what the National Rifle Association has to say, in general, on any particular issue involving guns, before the NRA even says it. Something like: enforce existing laws, of which there are plenty, no new restrictive gun laws are needed, the Second Amendment and armed self-defense is an individual, natural right and part of the heritage of a free people, gun crime is a problem because of a small criminal class that is being allowed to run wild, and gun ownership and use by responsible, law-abiding people prevents crimes and is generally beneficial. Everybody pretty much knows, too, the general argument of the NRA's counterpart, The Brady Campaign to Prevent Gun Violence (formerly Handgun Control Inc).

This line goes something like: gun violence is a problem because of the ready availability of guns in U.S. society, said guns behaving as a social pathogen, so commonsense laws need to be passed to restrict access to guns, and to keep our streets, homes, children and law enforcement officers safe, therefore any antigun law is a good law. So one knows the general thrust of virtually any Brady Center statement beforehand, too.

But what is one to think of a group called the American Hunters and Shooters Association? On its face it sounds like a pro-gun sporting group of hunters. Its website features homely, authentic-seeming, "folkish" photographs, e.g., a man in a hunter orange vest who regularly blogs on timely topics. AHSA identifies itself as a "national grass roots organization." The student researching a term paper or journalist working on a story might be pleased to find such a source. It offers press releases, which are prewritten news articles intended for journalistic use when writing news stories, and even connects to various other blogs where one can read or participate in discussions on gun safety and firearms laws. Behind this curtain of information, however, AHSA is neither grass roots, nor pro-gun, nor pro-hunting. Its "discussions" appear carefully modulated. Its estimated membership is only 150 people (NRA has more than 4 million), while the AHSA board consists of people connected to national anti-gun groups. It is a largely virtual front organization by which anti-gun propagandists attempt to distance themselves from their propaganda and which obviously tries to fragment electoral, behavioral unity among pro-gun groups by getting pro-gunners to vote for politicians with anti-gun voting records — politicians whom AHSA spends much effort promoting. Consider that an anti-gun politician can truthfully claim to be pro-Second Amendment simply by defining the Second Amendment as not applying to civilians. And these tactics apparently work, to some extent, for AHSA shows up as a source in news articles, especially around election times when reporters need political stories. It too will probably disappear when its tactical utility diminishes. The nice thing, from a propagandistic perspective, about a virtual organization however is that it can be activated and inactivated almost at will — and remain dormant until the circumstances require it again.

To illustrate how insidious indirect propagandas can be, back in the George H. W. Bush presidency the Drug Enforcement Administration made arrangements with Hollywood scriptwriters to insert anti-drug messages in scripts of movies and television shows. These were high-credibility sources habitually watched by people for whom these messages were intended.[99] Anti-gun groups have done the same with anti-gun messages, providing suggested story outlines to Hollywood scriptwriter guilds.

As a practical matter, it is virtually impossible to identify the true sources of information delivered by indirect means. Who has the time and energy? This is why it is such an effective technique. Propaganda scholars have called such information *grey propaganda,* where the source is hidden although the information may likely be true or subject to interpretation. *White propaganda,* meanwhile, is overt and more or less verifiable information from a known source, *Black propaganda* is disinformation, such as rumors, from an unknown source, front organization or fictional source. It is here that propaganda enters the realm of deliberate falsehoods. In the Iraq War, the U.S. military set up radio stations disguised as genuine Iraq stations to broadcast "news" to the Iraqi people, a very elaborate and deceptive front. A famous quote applies, variously attributed, "The first casualty of war is Truth."[100] A pack of lies, however, only takes the propagandist so far. Once credibility erodes, the propaganda becomes ineffective. See the Tenth Commandment concerning the use of truth in propaganda.

The code of ethics of the Public Relations Society of America, an organization whose members seem to strongly disapprove of the term "propaganda" when applied to their activities, forbids the use of dummy, front organizations. However, good public relations professionals can equivocate their way through any sticky ethical situation. In American politics, for example, use of such front organizations appears universal; fronts come and go regularly. The so-called "Citizen's Committee for Jones" invariably represents whatever party and interests the candidate belongs to. Much of this sort of activity is stimulated or made necessary by requirements of campaign finance laws that regulate expenditures by or on the part of candidates, but one should not fall prey to the naïve idea that merely regulating so-called "interest groups" will automatically render a pure and perfect world of

---

99 See A.B. Whitford and J. Yates, *Presidential Rhetoric and the Public Agenda: Constructing the War on Drugs* (Baltimore: Johns Hopkins University Press, 2009).

100 Much literature exists on this wartime use. The terms white, black and grey propaganda have been around for a long time; e.g., see Ellul; they are also mentioned in Doob, who is well worth reading.

political communication. At least with the interest groups disclosed, one may reasonably know from where the money and information comes and what purpose it presumably serves.

Sometimes front organizations are used for outright fraud. In the Michigan Republican convention of 2010, candidates from a "Tea Party" platform were put forward. It turned out that state Democrats had created this fake entity and candidates in an attempt to take votes away from strong candidates that the Democrats were leery of facing in the state election.

Facebook, blogs and other computer-assisted and social media have opened up new dimensions of indirect propaganda techniques. Online, it is relatively easy for propagandists to function like the professional agitators distributed clandestinely in a crowd, to excite, stimulate, introduce ideas, simulate public opinion, create a buzz, incite riot, without having to be overly involved and without knowledge of their true loyalties or intentions.

The universal practice of publicity offers another way of distancing the source from the propaganda. Publicity is when propagandists create synthetic news, a universal practice responsible for much if not most of the news that you see or hear. Even though we have wandered onto the turf of publicity, it deserves a separate chapter and therefore will be more properly discussed under Commandment Seven concerning Informational Accomodationism. Here, I will mention only the great value of publicity when considered as an indirect technique. When media "cover" a story that has been created and fed to them by publicity experts, the mere act of covering it invests it with an appearance of objectivity, like it "really happened," instead of being artificially contrived by a few PR people. Reading something in the newspaper or seeing it on television functions as an ultimate test of authenticity to some people. Media represent a higher, more glamorous reality to many—looming large: bigger, better and richer-seeming than their own comparatively innocuous lives. To actually be "in the newspaper" or "on television" is a peak experience of Life, a psychological-spiritual actualization of sorts, in another more vivid, higher dimension. If you don't believe this, see how many people come out of the woodwork when a television news camera appears, or how many lunch conversations are dominated by yesterday's news and entertainment broadcasts.

Think Tanks, Foundations
and Research Patronage

The number of so-called think tanks has increased over time, because they provide such an excellent mechanism for the delivery of indirect propaganda. The think tank or research institute is a dedicated, usually non-profit organization, that pursues some fairly specific line(s) of inquiry or social thought. Often it employs several scholars or "policy wonks" and may give paid fellowships to encourage resident intellectuals for periods of months or years, who are thus subsidized in their pursuit of the designated line of thought. Think tanks have various social-political bents: libertarian, free-market economics, liberal, conservative, and so on, all depending on where the money derives from. There is quite a thriving ecology of them. They manufacture knowledge that is injected at various points in the informational sociology, usually as "independent" research, ignoring the paradox that if the research is truly independent it would not be funded by a third party. The researcher becomes in effect a subcontractor carrying out or applying the social agenda of the think tank institute.

Lastly, funded "administrative research" by scientists and university researchers may function as an indirect propaganda technique for third-hand manufacture or stimulation of "friendly" information (remembering, of course, the principle that the enemy of your enemy is your friend). The technique relies also on what is essentially patronage. An RFP (request for proposal) solicits grant proposals to do research on a narrowly specified area. Grant proposals are reviewed by funding agencies, committees or representatives, who fund projects that will move forward the agenda of the patron organization. It sounds like independent research, and a case could be made for this, but what is really happening is that the researcher ends up as a contractor for the grantor after having promised a number of very specific deliverables in the grant proposal. Even endowed chairs at universities and centers may be similar — the fund provider has great leverage in specifying the sort of academics desired and type of research to be done. For example, a recent study shows that eating dark chocolate helps allay stroke damage. One need not wonder long where the funding originated. An ethical university or academic might reject such arrangements. Ambition, practicality and career advancement may override. Often, though, academics and funding sources share or align considerably on their interests and can work symbiotically together. Often, too, such research, although allegedly independent, has been bought and paid for, its conclusions decided on in advance. Academics and other beneficiaries of such patronage will defend themselves vigorously on this account. They are welcome to do so. Many are the social agendas pursued by such means. We live in an informational sociology of competing agendas. For this reason, patronage may be one of the best indirect techniques because it fosters the creation of agenda-favorable information.[101]

---

101 See Jack Walker's work on the role of patronage in interest group mobilization.

The Seventh Commandment

ACCOMMODATE INFORMATIONAL
NEEDS AND HABITS

"Informational accommodationism" means creating, packaging and distributing propaganda in ways that suit the informational needs and professional routines of journalists, editors, scriptwriters, interest groups, voluntary associations, churches, institutions, trade associations, corporations, blogs, news media, publishers, educators, researchers and various organizations that are in the business of creating, collecting and redistributing various kinds of specialized information to their markets or memberships. Of course, the propagandist furthers his own cause while doing so, for his motivation in providing such useful information is not charity.

Taking as an example the production of news, accommodationism works more or less like this. Journalists work in a deadline-driven industry. They must file stories on events in a timely fashion, often working on more than one story at a time. News, as in what is "new," is a perishable product that often needs to be knocked out in a hurry, often in competition with other information sources. Artistic craft enters in, of course, but timely delivery of a workmanlike product trumps artsy craft. In addition to these harsh marketing facts, journalists, being human, tend to efficiently take the path of least resistance when it comes to work, often snatching the "low-hanging" informational fruit; there being only so much time and energy available. Some people might describe this as laziness, but it is only business, often good business. News organizations need stories.

Propagandists know all this, for they are often themselves former journalists or have journalistic training. They have accordingly learned to create synthetic "news" to accommodate journalists. While naïve persons assume that news is something that just "happens," those in the know understand it as something that is often made to happen. There is a big difference. For the past hundred years or more, since the development of modern mass media systems, propagandists have provided pre-written news articles for the use of journalists. Today these are known as press releases. Also, propagandists provide background information (press kits), story opportunities, photo-ops, reports and synthetic spectacles suitable for broadcast, including press conferences and other structured, visually and informationally exciting events. Nowadays propagandists even "can" stories for television news, providing video footage that the local broadcaster can use either as is, or talk over as a so-called "B Roll." This information serves both journalist and propagandist. It also benefits the media organizations because fewer journalists are needed to process stories. In effect, propagandists subsidize news organizations.

In this way, the mountain can be made to come to Mohamed. The system can be very efficient. Every day thousands of press releases and story queries come to major newspapers and magazines. Estimates range on how much of the daily news comes from PR or "official" sources from about 50 to 80 percent. Of course, not all items are accepted or acceptable in so far as quality and news value. Small town newspapers and "local" media have much different content needs than big city media. Bigger items crowd out smaller items. Many press releases are so transparently self-serving as to be of no interest to a mass media audience. Some read as if written by idiots, so many, if not most, are rejected or ignored by editors. Even when accepted, facts contained or alleged need to be verified, for example, names and potentially libelous matters. At times, press releases are "picked up" and printed verbatim — or virtually so — while at other times press releases may simply help inform or suggest a story, or merely provide a quote. Most quotes from officials found in press releases are simply made up by the propagandists who write these releases, who of course know what needs to be said. I myself have done all this many times. I have also witnessed AP reporters working off a copy of a press release that they, for the most part, simply retyped and filed as a story. This happens frequently. Further, I have seen press releases that I had written reproduced almost in total under a journalist's byline. In fact, what would be called *plagiarism* in a university classroom is quite often called *journalism* throughout most of America. Even if it is not picked up verbatim, often the press release provides an idea, angle or a hermeneutic — an interpretation — of an event that will be absorbed and retransmitted by the journalist, thoughtlessly or intentionally. As you recall — since the propagandist is fundamentally in the extremely pragmatic business of interpreting the ongoing flux of reality so as to forward his own purposes — the adoption of a social interpretation may equate with a spectacularly visible sort of public success, while the propagandist remains invisible, which is probably where he is most effective. Thus, the propagandist's preferred interpretation of reality, also known as spin, may triumph over versions that are less attractive, more complicated or not judged as newsworthy. The proficient propagandist usually has a pretty good idea of newsworthiness and is more than willing to provide content.

Interest Groups

The vital importance of interests groups in the informational sociology of the United States must not be overlooked. In a large way, interests groups comprise the U.S. informational sociology. Interest groups represent large, organized systems with highly specialized informational needs and reach — they inform citizens, organizations, bureaucracies and politicians. For example, Mothers Against Drunk Driving hammers policy makers and police agencies with information, and has made drunk driving into the thriving industry that it is today, with heavy enforcement, check points, drunk schools and so forth.

For practical purposes interest groups can be thought of as specialized informational nodes,[102] absorbing, processing and distributing huge amounts of specialized data concerning their areas of concern. There are at least 40,000 or more interest groups and voluntary associations in the United States that are large enough to maintain formal addresses. A number have millions of individual members, while many more number in the hundreds of thousands, all actively united in some set of common concerns. Some are associations of member organizations, e.g., trade associations.

Virtually all interest groups regularly publish newsletters, magazines, send email notices to members, conduct publicity, operate websites and provide other services that may range from insurance discounts to legal defense. Providing this group of already motivated people with information relevant to them, people who by the mere act of joining together have shown themselves as informed and involved, almost guarantees social action in the desired direction — a main purpose of propaganda.

Sociologists and some PR professionals often speak of these groups as "publics." Note the plural. Pluralistic America especially is made up of many such publics concerned with more issues and topics than can be imagined,[103] some intensely weird, others more prosaic. Aiming propaganda at a mass audience is often wastefully ineffective, a shotgun approach that is expensive to boot, because the masses are more likely to be passively apathetic and inattentive to anything other than their food and gonads. But a true public, merely by virtue of the participatory high-involvement impulses of its many individual members, actively seeks and utilizes information. If the propagandist can find the right public, it will carry his message for him, amplifying and delivering it where it will do the most good. This is a question of alignment of interests. The propagandist customizes the pitch to suit the public. Senior associations may hear one version of reality, gun owners at a local sportsman club, another, and the local business association, a

---

102 Wright discusses this informational system approach in his book *Interest Groups & Congress.* He states that interest groups function as information nodes that can be considered as being in the business of collecting and processing information and *strategically* redirecting it to where it will do the most good, e.g. congressmen and policy makers, by means of lobbying, media, attention publics, regulatory agencies. Some groups inform police agencies, for example Mothers Against Drunk Driving.

103 An eye-opening exercise is to examine the Gale Research *Encyclopedia of Associations.*

third. Likewise, churches, another form of voluntary association, often have their own newsletters, electronic or hardcopy, usually badly in need of content. Alumni magazines and associations provide another channel. Bureaucracies and corporations also have manifold informational needs, as do local libraries and community groups, e.g., speakers and lecture series. How many times have you seen local non-profit organizations, which we must not forget are as enriching to their managers as are for-profit organizations, glom on to organizational newsletters, whose editors are glad to run such content because it takes up space while creating an impression of selfless community service?

Informal networks are useful as well, even though they may be largely invisible on the surface of things. Various ego and social needs drive gossip — the need to be perceived by self and others as in the know — so by understanding and accommodating the informational needs of gossip and informal networks, the propagandist can permeate an organization with his ideas. Rumors can destroy ideas and reputations by prejudgment as well as undermine or prop up morale.

Professional and social networks also play into the accommodation of informational needs. The easy familiarity of left-leaning National Public Radio's many current events talk shows, for example, suggests a business plan of promotion-via-networking more than "objective" news. It seems every "guest" has a new book or represents an organization out to save the world (at public or government expense, of course). The talk shows on the so-called Conservative Right are no different in their promotion of products and programs — except the social/professional networks activated are not quite the same.

As has been the case throughout this book, in practice the Commandments will often overlap. Accommodation of informational needs can also be regarded as a good way of controlling the flow of information, i.e., the First Commandment. Accommodationism is so pervasive — although often subterranean — that it deserves special consideration. Accommodationism functions as the ether through which propaganda is transmitted. It carries the word.

The Eighth Commandment

ADDRESS PSYCHOLOGICAL, SPIRITUAL & SOCIAL NEEDS

Propaganda must speak to primal psycho-spiritual and social needs that in the modern age have so often been vacated because of the waning influence of religion, family and traditional cultural roles.

The basic idea here is that the modern, mass society media baby, who ranges in age from about eight to eighty years, is a curious hybrid of neurotic insecurity and solipsistic egomania. More or less rootless, more slavish consumer than efficacious citizen, he lacks meaningful gut-level social orientation or a firm sense of identity, place, belonging or personal power. Mass society leaves him wanting, unsatisfied in fundamental ways. This especially applies to the young. Instead of enduring, comforting orientation it merely provides — always for a fee — over-stimulation via an unending stream of ersatz need-substitutes, deceits large and small, easy to obtain, but lacking in spiritual nourishment. Although drowning in sugary media representations that substitute for meaning, he still craves meat.

The modern clichés of "finding oneself" or "having an identity crisis" would probably have struck people from traditional societies as absurd. In fact, they still do, because people from more or less traditional societies yet walk amongst us: immigrants from less "developed" places of the world and the social "backwaters" of America. Some people still raise their children "in person," talk with them, transmit stories, traditions and work/life skills, and do not simply consign them to the mass-institutional indoctrination systems of public education and mass media.[104] People from traditional societies know who they are because a social context largely defines them, or at the least provides a solid foundation for identity. Consider here the historical "John the Carpenter," whose son and father were carpenters and whose great grandchildren many times over still live today. But the modern Carpenters, by no means carpenters or anything so definite, are first publicly funded students for up to 16 or more years, a role that socializes them for employment within the state. Then they become working, tax-paying homo-units who must somehow scramble for whatever living and sense of identity, self-worth and place they can find. Failing at this, they may become clients of the state — convicts, welfare recipients or homeless (who still receive state benefits). The descendants are adrift, alone in the crowd — yet another cliché used to describe the situation of the modern individual. To provide a supporting anecdote, I have talked to quite a few university students who have no idea what their parents really do at work.

There is a maddening paradox, however, that is parcel to the mass society kind of life. While functionally only a homo-unit, the mass individual is socialized to think himself unique and inviolable. His vote, and therefore his opinion, means everything to himself and the society — so he has been socialized, and has probably convinced himself that this is so, with help from propagandists who act as vote-herds. He has an opinion on everything — which is amazing. By his vote or opinion he is listened to and matters in the big scheme of things, just as God and all the saints once upon a time were thought to have listened intimately to the prayers of each and every person. According to the self-help books that sell so well — because people so desperately need help and orientation — the mass individual is potentially anything and

---

104 The "Developed World" in the modern sociological vocabulary apparently means the most effectively propagandized segments.

everything he really wants to be. But isn't this as much as saying he is nothing at all in particular?[105] He has been conditioned to think of himself as a sacred, special, unique individual, as have several hundred million others more or less just like him within a standard deviation or so. This is the paradox — the person who is everything, equipped with inalienable rights to pursue happiness, the ego at world's center, who is at the same time nothing other than a job, and perhaps not even that.

Negating the nothingness thus becomes a main drive of modern life. Reconciling logical opposites on such a scale can only be accomplished by protean propaganda. Formed to suit any situation, an infinitely renewable resource, propaganda fills Life's many holes with words, images, stories, orientation and meaning.

Every person can also be viewed as a bundle of base-level animal needs. How to propagandistically address corporeal needs is usually obvious — e.g., promises of food, sex, shelter, or blame directed at those people and things responsible for shortages. There is little reason to review such matters here other than to note that the hungry, fearful or anxious individual can often be motivated to action more easily by agitation propagandas than a person whose basic material needs are filled. This is why Marxist guerillas in some areas of the world have killed relief workers — the Marxists believed that desperation led more quickly to a proper revolutionary state of mind. Likewise, bad economic times make for cargo-cult mass-democratic politics — incantation and ritual unaccompanied by genuine productive work — consider here the superficial vagueness of the prayer-like programs of the Obama presidential machinery. Also, appeals to self-interest such as economic programs, lower taxes (except for "the rich"), better neighborhoods, etc., are obvious enough, too, where little discussion is required despite the universality of such needs. As long as someone else, or an ungraspable abstraction (e.g., "corporations"), is paying the bill, these are relatively easy needs to exploit. Given that bellies are full, psycho-spiritual needs move to the fore, although they are not unconnected to the realm of guts and gonads.[106] Still, they apply more to the human being as a social animal that transcends the solitary beast.

---

105 A man told me, "I thought I knew who I was once, but it turned out that I was mistaken when the next fad came along."

106 Don't imagine that I am some disembodied academic who floats through life. I am all for guts and gonads in proper measure.

Need categories might be roughly grouped into overlapping clusters that I will discuss with as much precision as I can muster. These clusters are *identity*, which includes ego, power and personal efficacy; *meaning*, which covers issues such as understanding the world, where it is going and political anxiety resulting from the absence of the assurances inherent in concrete explanations; and *belonging*, which is feeling wanted, useful, as if one has a real place or satisfying role in the world or a tangible social unit.

For the sake of common sense, I will try to avoid dependence on psychological jargon because much of it is tautological anyway — for example, the psychologist explains that people join groups because of a deep-seated social need to join groups, or they must have sex because of the sex drive. Professional liturgical jargon may make such talk seem profound, but such smoke is not illumination. One must sympathize with the descriptive difficulties involved in any attempt to map these areas because the spiritual, psychological and social realms lack clear demarcations. Description becomes at best probabilistic, covering generalities and confounded impulses, perceptions and misperceptions, and becomes increasingly fuzzy as we try to broaden the description to take in more events. Nevertheless, experientially dense cores lie hidden in these fuzzy-seeming descriptions. I settle for merely describing the situation and some of the main propaganda techniques that rise up in response to the seemingly general situation.

Identity, Ego and Power

A line by J.R.R. Tolkien asks, "Who are you, alone, in the dark?" This is quite the question, for which I know not the answer. One just *is*.

In the everyday sense, identity appears to be a thing built in social contexts and carried through various other contexts, in somewhat modified forms. At least this seems usual, or maybe inborn character is indeed destiny. [107] Or biology. A hard kernel of self seems to survive over time — but this may be a retrospectively projected illusion. I don't believe identity is as well understood as some imagine. Sometimes we surprise not only ourselves but others too. In the case here, suitable for

---

107 But I certainly don't recognize the raging adolescent who once inhabited my body and left incoherent scrawls (and an occasional good sentence) in various notebooks many years ago.

purpose of this discussion, identity is a sense of the nature of self: who and what you really are, or should be, or shouldn't be, and who or what you are definitely not.

The mass society individual, again, being all that he can be — that is to say nothing in particular — needs to largely shift for himself concerning the long-term bother of developing and realizing his own sense of identity. Propaganda, however, offers readymade identities that save all the trouble of building one from scratch. Many people take this easy way. Such conveniences come at a price, however, which beyond becoming someone's fool, is neglecting more substantive self-development. Organized religions, political parties and organized social movements are common sources of identity. So are mass media products. And so is "culture;" which equates with saying that available identity concepts are floating around, handy for use, e.g., patriotism, ethnic and national identity, transnational new world identity, cool cat, manly man, green environmental sustainability and so forth. There is no shortage of options that propagandists can pluck from the trees when needed. In this regard, propaganda appears once again to be an infinitely renewable resource that responds to a boundless market.

An example: Mr. Xmith, we shall call him, a white male, 60, listens to talk radio daily as well as watches the sorts of political commentary/entertainment shows that have been disguising themselves as television news now for several years. His small talk deals with national, world and historical events. He speaks of presidents and prime ministers as if he dined with them last evening and knew their minds and characters. Economics and world politics are his intimates. Listening to him try to monopolize a conversation reminds of Hitler's famous dinner "conversations," in which the Führer regaled his admiring guests with views on various subjects. Xmith rants to anyone who will listen (not many) arguing "his" cause. He is outraged that the country is descending into decay, after a glorious history of technological, economic and social accomplishment. "Liberals" and "socialists" have taken over. He identifies celebrity enemies and denounces individual politicians, as if he had personal vendettas with them. He is a failure at careers (having somehow managed to get fired from a civil service professional position), multiple marriages and life in general. He drinks himself unconscious at night while watching DVDs of westerns and combat television shows from the 1950-1960 era, symbolic of the strong, white male ruling the earth. Even his car is pointed in this direction — an aging

Buick. His talk is a prayer directed at everything he is not. Working a meaningless job, despite considerable technical training, not making much money, lacking the social skills to conduct professional business, he poses as a master of all things economic and cultural. He scans magazines and watches old movies from which he gleans factoids that serve him as assertions. Generally disregarded and powerless, even by his own family, he constantly evokes images of regard and power, e.g., national respect. The gulf between his social actuality and his status claims is unbridgeable except by the propaganda that he needs more than Prozac to manage anxiety and the terror of his meaninglessness. In his adopted, powerful identity, Xmith Prime we might call it, agendas and rhetoric echo the national and world politics content of the talk show programming he exposes himself to daily. Instead of a sad, solitary failure, the man without a date on the horizon, the Xmith Prime identity stands as the lonely hero of a superior lost culture, a last Mohican of the American Golden Age political economy. Absurd pretensions take on larger meanings, historical tones and a noble superiority of character instead of a powerless flyspeck. Xmith Prime's identity appears derived both from media products and from flattering political and mass educational socialization appeals. He is, at last, important in his own mind. However, sadly, all this nonsense predetermines his future developmental trajectory; his personality is limited, a caricature rather than a man, because he has abandoned whatever native good sense he may have had, and taken up instead this flattering new interpretation of the world. One can from now on pretty much predict what he will have to say on any issue, probably forever. He has arrived, developmentally speaking.

It is just as easy to pick an example of an adopted cliché leftist identity. Associate professor ZJones performs as the outspoken champion of the downtrodden, whomever and wherever they may happen be, although they seem never to be around to speak for themselves. She regards university teaching as praxis in the Marxist sense. The latter means she is supposed to teach sociologically correct thought and behavior in order to accelerate class-based social change and "the struggle" of historical progress. ZJones' classes are ideological indoctrination sessions, she being indoctrinator and judge. Gender neutrality is demanded in use of pronouns; a "his" in the wrong place perpetuates gender oppression. A perceived conservative view results in lower grades because it is by definition incorrect thought. Although allegedly opposed to authority, one gets the impression that ZJones very much would like to be authority, enforcing thought and conduct codes, drawing the reluctant into a better future where every resource is meted out via progressive programs, under supervision of intelligentsia like herself. At committee meetings, whatever the topic, one can count on ZJones to speak out for the needs of minority students and "people of color" (she is lily white and lives in the very whitest of suburbs), and how policies such as admission standards discriminate. Always occupying the moral high ground, she stands for world peace, disarmament, non-smoking, and against private gun ownership, patriarchy (but not the good old gal networks that dominate the college landscape) and big business. Her idea of a seminar on social justice is to take students to visit convicts whom she sees as victims of class struggle rather than transgressors and malefactors. Although publishing little scholarship, she protests often in letters and declamations, speaking on behalf of social justice. Her view of history is a tale of class, race and gender repression opposed by righteous revolutionary collectives. She teaches something she calls "social thought" which seems to demonstrate her state of moral elevation on various topics. One can predict what she will have to say on virtually any issue. Her Volvo — she wouldn't be seen driving an American car — displays a half dozen prescriptive bumper stickers: e.g., "The best man for the job is most often a woman", "You can't hug your child with nuclear arms", "Think globally, act locally", and "eracism." Nonalignment with ZJones thought is immoral. Professionally and socially she associates with people who think just like her. They cohere as a superior in-group. As a humanities professor, she also considers herself above professors who teach business and sciences because she is in engaged in teaching people how to live and what to value, while they merely impart technical skills.

   Both Xmith and ZJones exemplify what Jacques Ellul has called "psychological crystallization." This is a long-term propaganda effect where a person ceases to grow on his own accord and becomes, instead, a creature of propaganda. It's the psycho-spiritual equivalent to foot binding.

   On the surface, these two persons seem opposite, but underneath, they are much the same. Propaganda has taken over. It has given them a feeling of certainty and superiority of intellect and morals, and alignment with movement politics. This includes history itself, for both are agents of what they see as historical forces, progressively liberal and conservatively traditional. Both can now think themselves smart, too, as do most people, as this seems a common and perhaps necessary form of mental hygiene; but this sort of absolutism is another thing altogether. Creative independent judgment has been exchanged for a petrified illusion of self-importance, direction and orientation. Propagandistic clichés compensate for inner growth. They have stopped thinking, as they now imagine themselves to sufficiently understand, and to have the universe pinned down for them like a butterfly in a collection. They can achieve this level of unfreedom only through propaganda. Withdraw propaganda and their propped-up egos would have to face a most unpleasant reality—the self, in the dark, alone. In looking over these case studies, I remember George Orwell's phrase about "smelly little orthodoxies." To his description I would add the word "suffocating."

To the extent it credibly feeds a desperate ego, propaganda is accepted; Jacques Ellul would say that it is demanded. Vanity, self-importance, ultimate meanings that support a vital personal role in the universe, all these things must be present in the identity-based worldview offered by propaganda. They are in all the great propagandas that have been used to control and justify elite dominations in the name of the common good. The humility of an alleged good Christian may be merely an inverse vanity: "I am the most humble person in the world." Sending missionaries to the heathens in foreign parts resonates of imagined, spiritual-moral superiority as much or more than charity, especially when there are less exotic fools and heathens living just down the street who could benefit from missionary work as much as anyone. As for a chosen people or elect predestined to salvation, how much more ego-centered can one get? God — the intelligence informing the universe — has entered into a lopsided contract with one's ego, a microscopic worm that inhabits an infinitesimal cranny? I do not reject religious concepts here, but only call attention to their common abuse in propaganda based on the fact that they can easily be morphed into flattering self-delusions.

In practice, what propagandists do rather than invent new orientations and worldviews, a most difficult long-term task, is to pick up bits and pieces of things that are culturally available, laying about, and reflect them back in a more focused manner. This kind of symbolic recycling was discussed under the Second Commandment which calls for propagandists to reflect the values and extant beliefs of the audience. In so doing, the propagandist is conscious of the desperate egomaniacs comprising the audience.

Consumerism

Consumerism offers other easy and popular ways to address identity demands. All one needs is money or, better yet — skipping over the laborious step of earning money — easy credit.

The consumer can now obtain an identity simply by purchasing its central key symbolic components and paraphernalia. Consider Mr. Office Worker Man who fancies to become a fly fisherman. He goes to one of several popular sporting goods stores that purvey such identities. He acquires most or all of the following: a subscription to a fly fishing magazine, waders, a special fly fisherman's hat, polarized sun glasses to best see fish underwater, a bamboo handcrafted fly rod, a folding case for flies, a few dozen hand tied flies with exotic names like "Blue Dunn" and which suggest an arcane Gnosticism of hidden lore and secret joys, leaders, tapered lines, line dressing, special felt bottom wading shoes that don't slip on mossy rocks, a khaki vest with many pockets and sheepskin wool plackets to attach flies, books and videos demonstrating the art, classes and seminars on fly fishing techniques and fly tying, a fly-tying kit equipped with silk flosses, thread, tinsel, peacock tail feathers, golden pheasant and jungle cock capes and grizzly rooster hackles, an outfitter-guided trip to allegedly great fly fishing streams of Wyoming and Montana, and maybe even the special edition, sportsman, four-wheel-drive vehicle that can get him into the back country but which will sit in the parking lot at the office for fifty weeks of the year. All this will cost thousands and there is not necessarily even a fish involved. Assuming the consumer-angler can even catch a fish, he may opt for special "catch and release" fly fishing in designated streams, a practice that supposedly frees the fish undamaged (I doubt this) after the artful catch. So obviously he is not just a hungry brute, but an artist seeking transcendent perfection who eschews the lower functions of killing and eating. Also packaged in the sale is a whiff of something primal, recalling hunting and gathering, and an association with a love of nature and the outdoors, which at some point may flutter off into an animistic sort of spirituality accompanied by the ceremonies of the fly fishing art. Correct form alone may be sufficient unto itself for the true artist. Several movies portray variants of the mystical perfectionism of fly fishing, which is not only a return to the imagined joys of Nature, but a sort of Zen moment where the Universe and the Self arrive at the same moment with roll cast, ripple and the aesthetically perfect fish. It is this demonstration of higher aesthetic class that puts the fly fisherman above and beyond the good-old-boy type of fisherman out for a catfish to fry. In Western America one sees many such expensively clad men with significant disposable incomes flailing away with custom fly rods on the more picturesque waters. Conveniently, too, the same chain stores that purvey these exhaustive lines of identity-products also have their own identity-enhancing credit cards, decorated with naturalistic outdoor scenes of leaping fish and other game animals. Delay in gratification is eliminated wherever possible — one does not have to work for years to become a true master, all one needs is to buy the stuff. A behavioral conditioning is underway — the act of buying itself satisfies the impulse to excel, reinforcing the identity that when threatened by failure resorts to buying even more stuff.

It should be apparent that the real product consumed here is an identity and the cluster of traits subsumed within this concept. That special aesthetic of fly fishermen that distinguish them from lesser mortals and fishermen appeals to Vanity. Fishing becomes Art, an ineffable and mystically tinged experience. Mr. Office Worker transfigures, elevated above his peers, closer to perfection and nature through his purchases. The more high-end paraphernalia he buys the better he becomes, in his mind, even if he only practices his fly-casting on the front lawn so his neighbors can also experience his artfulness.

Lucrative industries are built around the false instant identity syllogism: great performers use product X; you can use X; therefore you will be a great performer. Consider the implied promise of the athletic shoe company that advertises, "Just do it" and named after the goddess of victory. For $150 one can associate oneself with winners while skipping all physical and mental bother. Or consider the brewing companies whose advertisements syllogistically imply that large-breasted beautiful women flock to the drinkers of their beer. Likewise, the would-be hunter purchases, at three times the normal cost, "premium" ammunition with ballistic capabilities to strike a target out to 500 yards, even though he cannot hit a bushel basket consistently at 50 yards given the best match grade rifle and ammunition in the world. Then, there is the person who buys the $8,000 artist's signature guitar yet can barely play a C chord. Identity appeals imply quick and easy mastery — an accomplished ego worthy of respect — a superiority not worked for, but demanded by an ego so needy that it gobbles up even imaginary merit. Such behaviors could also be attributed to the need for power or personal efficacy. The word "hobby" is not used much anymore in consumer appeals because it detracts from the implied promise of mastery through consumerism; a hobby being only a small thing, while the needs of the power-starved ego are vast. Plus, identity marketing has a cyclical causality operating within it — if at first one doesn't succeed, then one buys better equipment. Any existential inadequacy recalled by failure brings about more consumer behavior in an attempt to find a remedy. This applies to all manner of desirable properties and excellences, e.g., beauty, strength, intelligence, wealth (or its appearance at any rate), sexual attractiveness, and so forth. As the Preacher said, vanity of vanities; all is vanity.

Meanings, Routines and Rituals

Chaos is an unattractive prospect. Even those who claim to be anarchists and nihilists do not really seek chaos — rather they tend to see in chaos a cleansing force that will wipe away a current status quo they feel must be rejected. In other words, they see in chaos the return of a higher, more wholesome natural order, a liberating potential for a better world. Hilariously, the blackest nihilist is usually a romantic at heart.

On the whole, people doggedly expect and benefit from a certain order in life, e.g., routines, direction, a sense of purpose, a comfortable safe place to sleep, friends they can feel superior to and comfortable with, the knowledge that regular feedings, pay or social security checks will continue, that everything is getting better all the time, and so on. Even the most unassuming persons hope to find in the idea of an orderly life a predictably comfortable safe zone — "I am just a regular hard working guy with a family. I go to work and pay my taxes." Adopting such a stance removes much anxiety about life insofar as the individual's external situation, the bubble, remains stable. When the situation becomes unstable propaganda must be pumped in.

Beyond ego needs concerning power and personal vanity, people therefore seek out and welcome assurances of an orderly rational world with predictable outcomes. Attending to the daily news is one way that fills emptiness; it also soothes fear of the unknown and the known by making things seem predictable. Sociologist Herbert Gans observed that a major content theme found in the daily national news is the return to normalcy. News reassures. Don't worry, is the implied message, for appropriate authorities are working on the problem that threatens us. We'll keep you updated.

In this regard, news and the corporate communications to which so many are exposed daily convey propaganda that functions like the old time watchman, who in doing nightly rounds would cry out the intervals, "eleven o'clock and all is well," thus assuring any who might lay awake worrying in their beds. Likewise, the chief executive gives the annual state-of-the-corporate-entity speech as an assurance to everyone aboard that the corporate ship is still on course, despite a few delays, avoidable icebergs, and the fuel shortage. All is well, or will be soon, under this administration.

These kinds of ritualistic communication answers existential threats of disorder. Corporate speeches often say very little in terms of specific content. I heard one recently in which the great leader talked about "vision" and "how well we are positioned to make this an even better organization" and how "we will move confidently into the future." The address had fewer specifics than most fortune cookies. By filling in the blanks with the suitable proper names, it could have been given almost anywhere to any corporate audience. It seemed to reassure the intended audience quite well, however — they were apparently hearing what they were expecting to hear. The speaker didn't really say anything other than the modern, corporate version of "eleven o'clock and all is well," which in this case was a very doubtful proposition. Such rituals soothe, however, like a mass in Latin that virtually nobody understands in terms of content. Relax. The current administration is in charge and God is in heaven above.

Having witnessed perhaps 100 such speeches over the course of my professional life delivered by governors, lieutenant governors, presidents, university presidents, corporate leaders and others on various occasions, the following formula is the most common underlying text: everything has been good in the past, it is good now, and will be even better in the future. Consider how this compares to "As it was in the beginning it is now and forever shall be, amen." I bet you never knew politicians were so religious.

The same may be true of staff and committee meetings that take place essentially for the sake of meeting rather than as a means to achieve a tangible result. In academia, the meeting is often the end product. As I heard it put once in a governmental context: "The purpose of that meeting was to have that meeting." This ritual aims to banish disorder and simulate management or control of events. We get together and chant the blah-blah prayer. It alleviates the existential panic that wells up when things are perhaps too quiet. The sound and fury become ritualistic.

Belonging

Returning to the basic needs of the paradox-ridden egomaniac human, this same individual who sees himself the center of all things, wishes to feel as if he were immersed in something larger and more contextually meaningful than himself. Beyond seeing regard for himself reflected in the eyes of others, a great need, he also seeks a sense of genuine belonging. This is feeling wanted, useful or needed, as if he has a significant place or indispensable role in a world outside himself, a world that he experiences as a series of jarring bumps and clatters intruding on his solipsism. Here, of course, we butt up against territory also described by the Fourth Commandment which deals with the use of groups to "horizontally" shape beliefs and behaviors. The horizontal propaganda of groups and small groups indeed offers this sense of belonging, always at the price of alignment with the goals of the propagandists that design such groups.

It is not enough that an individual feel personally accomplished. It must be in a context of something bigger than himself. For example, a professor may be very accomplished in a field, and likes to think himself the agent of transmission of western culture, a torchbearer of sorts. He belongs, therefore, to this larger noble endeavor, a discipline that has collectively waged war against the darkness for centuries, of course with varying degrees of success and many setbacks. He is part of an ongoing priesthood. Other professors may see themselves as agents of a progressivism that rejects an oppressive past. In either case, however, they are aligned with tectonic historical forces and social movements. The professor works for the future while representing the past. This idea of working for the future and past, in spite of administrative Philistines who cheapen university education, keeps professors invested in their jobs and allows them to rationalize away the many incongruities facing them.

The ideas of *belonging* and *continuity* manifest in ways beyond count in propagandistic use of themes such as patriotism, nationalism, ethnicity, race (which in days of old was a term that included family and extended tribe), religion, culture (to the extent culture is conscious), family, institutions such as universities and their time-and-space-spanning body of alumni, tradition, and the U.S. Marines and its fraternity of graduates. These are just a few. One of the great appeals of Roman Catholicism, for a particularly good example, is its institutional respectability. The organization dates back more than a millennium — it says more than two — connecting the lonely individual to an unbroken stream of endeavor, to meaning and to an absolute cosmic order. No wonder people jump in and submerge themselves, including many intellectuals for whom Catholicism offers many satisfying opportunities to explain the pirouettes of angels on the heads of pins, a direct participation in a rich intellectualist history. All this is available for the price of Easter duty. This beats being alone in the dark.

Or the individual can join the Peace Corps, or become part of the budding Sustainability Movement — a fad that will carry humanity into a sustainable future, although I have no clear idea what the term "sustainability" really indicates. (I think this lack of clarity is also true of many who claim to pursue sustainability.) They thereby become part of something larger than themselves that promises to affect ultimate outcomes. For their own benefit it might be best if they inquired no further, assuming they seek comfort in such an easily won sense of higher purpose.

Propaganda works by offering the needy mass society individual vivid and easily accessible senses of identity, meaning and belonging. Address these basic psycho-spiritual needs.

The Ninth Commandment

PERSONALIZE AND DEHUMANIZE
AS APPROPRIATE

Personalization/dehumanization is the attachment of characteristics and personality traits to individuals, groups, animals and
things, in such ways as to make them more or less sympathetic
or unsympathetic. Dehumanization metaphorically transforms people
into infernal things such as plagues, machines, monsters, animals or
simply into things or parts of things.

In its extremes, a personalization treatment may itself become a
total symbol, summing the hopes and hates bound up in some broad
social phenomenon into a single myth-like symbolic personality: e.g.,
Hitler, Tojo, Osama Bin Laden, Mao, Abraham Lincoln, Martin Luther
and Martin Luther King, all of whom were propagandistically elevated
to supreme villains or heroes (or both) and thus came to symbolize
very different things to different sets of people.

There are two possible ways to go about personalization/dehu-
manization: positively or negatively. A reciprocal or complementary
relationship often exists between them, where a group, person or

thing that is being promoted receives positive personalization treatment, while another group, the perceived enemy or the opposition, receives negative treatment. For example, all social movements that I am aware of have their heroes and villains. The very same person whom adherents perceive as a martyr, and therefore the recipient of glowing personalization treatments, may receive extreme negative treatments from political or social opponents. One faction's saint is another's deviant criminal agitator, e.g., Martin Luther King as a symbol very soon came to transcend the actual man — and many other dedicated men and women — to personify the civil rights movement. The United States now has dozens of Martin Luther King Boulevards; but in his time King was often treated as a Negro Communist agitator, terms having extremely negative connotations back in that era.

Personalization occurs quite naturally via everyday language, symbolic or spoken. People seem to automatically personalize and dehumanize, without any apparent thought whatsoever; and it probably works so very well as a propaganda technique because it well suits the usual heedlessness of everyday life.

Personalization and dehumanization also help in adhering to the Third Commandment of Propaganda — to disambiguate — because in practice they help artificially polarize real or imagined differences between people and the policies they represent so as to achieve that simplistic cartoon worldview that is a hallmark of an effective propaganda.

Positive and Negative Personalization

Positive use of personalization or humanization attributes characteristics seen as virtuous, praiseworthy or admirable.[108] It invests people, animals and things with the widely recognized better traits of humankind. Roughly speaking, the more such traits the higher the person, thing or object places in humanistic evaluation. Positive personalization propaganda might depict members of racial, ethnic or friendly ingroups as being loving, community-centered, beautiful, responsible, cultured, smart, forthright, happy, noble, trustworthy, hard working,

---

108 Both terms have been used. The apparent king of humanization and dehumanization scholarship is Haig Bosmajian. His *The Language of Oppression* is a quick and enlightening read.

honorable, generous, talented, creative, beautiful, environmentally-conscious, in touch with nature and so forth. The list is endless and is drawn from the store of values and beliefs cherished by the audience, beliefs also reflected in mass media entertainment and news. For example, a respectful, black teenager might be shown on his way home from the school for the gifted while helping an old lady cross the street; or the politician may be shown as charismatic, glowing with health, benign intent, wisdom and family values manifested in the form of an attractive wife and children that accompany him while on stage. One might also look to the beatifying accounts written by political camp followers on their leaders, for example, the Kennedy family of politicians or President Ronald Reagan. Deliberate legend-building of this sort often passes for neutral reporting.

To emphasize, don't overlook that the average reader or viewer seldom has reason to finely sift for the contaminating elements in a description. Heedless absorption seems more the rule. Repeated often enough, such personalization treatments may become unquestioned facts. Also, personalization translates the sociologically abstract into something more akin to gossip, which makes matters much more understandable to those many people who seem to traffic in this style of communication.

Negative personalization or dehumanization of people or things attributes undesirable and decidedly non-virtuous attributes worthy of censure; provoking disgust, outrage, enmity; robbing people of essential humanity; makes them seem evil, crazy, uncultured or stupid. In a word, they are painted as a bad lot. Here we may see people portrayed variously as inhumane, ugly, cheap, criminal, irresponsible, greedy, violent, crude, sneaky, undemocratic, bullying, vermin, uncaring about animals, the environment or, worse yet, as its active destroyers. As ever, the list of possible negative traits and comparisons appears endless, and is drawn from that which is widely devalued and detested by the intended audience, from inverse values. People may also be compared to machines or vice versa, but with negative connotation, e.g., "He was a regular garbage disposal." In negative counterparts to the examples just presented above, a foul-mouthed black teenage high school dropout may be shown mugging an old lady for her social security check; or the whore-mongering politician with his gin-blossom nose sleazes after a bribe to vote for a project that will enrich cronies while hastening the extinction of a rare species of rain forest snails. It used to be that the lecherous villain in black was shown tying the beautiful, white-gowned blonde heroine on the railroad tracks, but fashions in absolute evil have slowly changed as new administrative/managerial issues have been injected into the informational sociology. Now the overall-wearing, shotgun-toting, white southern male intimidates the idealistic volunteer election worker.

In its purest applications, dehumanization removes a person to beyond the perimeter of human sympathy. This is often accomplished through *objectification* via scientific description. Thus, a young man in the forensic psychiatric center who writes regularly to his mother can be scientifically described as, "The subject exhibited writing behavior." He now impinges on consciousness merely as set of symptoms rather than a person, and anything that may be done to him, accordingly, is merely "treatment" that transcends justice or injustice. We must feel virtuous, reluctantly of course, at having deprived him of his liberty, but there was really no choice. For only the mentally healthy can have liberty. The mentally ill person must be protected from himself, while society must be protected from the mentally ill; although few ever care to look at the matter in such stark terms. The use of dehumanization makes this sort of moral judgment unnecessary, however. Casting every act or thought of a person as a symptom or behavioral manifestation of some dread disorder robs a person of humanity, and even the dignity of possessing that defining human attribute of free will. Such a person instantly transforms into merely "a case," presumably part of an administrative "case load." He must be "helped." The "subject" can now be prescribed, by court order if necessary, whatever treatment is currently in vogue, such as whipping, lobotomy, psychotropic drugs, time out or continued imprisonment — all of which have had their seasons at various times when employed by scientifically informed authorities. A preferred way of treating political dissidents in the Soviet Union in its later years, for instance, was to commit them to mental hospitals. A preoccupation with freedom or dislike of an oppressive government thus officially became a mental condition. Likewise, when violence is defined as "an epidemic" any humanistic element disappears altogether. Such language invites clinical intervention. The language of collectivism similarly justifies permeation of all social levels by a state authority in the interests of the collective. Quasi-scientific language removes the human factor on both sides of the coercive equation. Even more useful to propagandists is how easy it becomes to spin visions based on the epistemological assumptions of this sort of dehumanizing language. Plausible cant just rolls off the bureaucratic tongue.

Even so-called Attention Deficit Disorder (ADD) is most frequently used, I suspect, to justify increased bureaucratic control over children and their parents by means of elevating natural, childlike traits into symptoms. The result is that an ineffective administration can look heroic, fighting the problem at its imagined roots, all while not accomplishing much of anything substantial, as managing a drugged child is certainly easier than the hard, individual-level work required to teach the child to read and think.

The clinical, dehumanized type of power relationship underscores another reason why dehumanization works so well as a propaganda and mobilization technique — it allows instantaneous distancing psychologically, emotionally and even morally from acts, victims and mistakes. It erases any doubt or ambiguity that might otherwise keep one awake at night, such as drugging a child. One could well argue that such emotional distancing is necessary to maintain a modern, professional relationship with the patient. And it probably is. I leave this argument to others.

Use of Dysphemisms and Euphemisms in Personalization

That garden-variety rhetorical technique, the euphemism, literally a "good-ism," is also good for psychologically diffusing any discomfort that may be caused by the too-direct use of language.

Rather than killed, the nasty, smelly, old poodle is "put down" or "euthanized." A person killed may become "collateral damage" or a "target" that had to be "neutralized." Euphemistic language buffers the essential ugliness of hard action and conditions such that the issuing authority may appear downright altruistic.

The dysphemism is merely a reverse euphemism. It is a "bad-ism," a word with negative connotations. A voluntary association of people becomes "a clan;" freedom fighters, "insurgents;" the place where they live, a "compound;" a person arrested, a "perp" or "person of interest;" and a "big boned" person, "fat." Applying dysphemisms to designate persons or groups as "at-risk" or "suspected terrorists" may justify perpetual surveillance, suspension of rights or extra-constitutional intervention. Conversely, the proper euphemism elevates them to desperate heroes fighting against impossible odds, martyrs or freedom fighters.

When defined and applied operationally, as an administrative protocol or legal definition, the bureaucratic euphemism/dysphemism can mean almost anything that happens to be administratively convenient, e.g., "at risk" becomes a checkmark designation on a form that may justify home invasion, i.e., "intervention" and monitoring by state social workers. If challenged, the administrator may resort to other protocols designed to protect "patient" or "client" rights. The application of such a moralistic tint also dehumanizes, for the patient is no longer a person but a "case" of bureaucratically defined rights. (See also Commandment Eleven on the necessity of demonstrating ethics and morals in propaganda.) The term "patient" is in itself a dehumanization that encourages psychological and moral distance. Such lexical games especially play to the advantage of the bureaucrat-administrator who controls the flow of information. Persons lacking access to the events that are being thus (mis)described usually cannot see just how arbitrarily contrived such word choices may be. The administrative mill is always in need of grist — for its existence must be somehow justified objectively — and, thus, there is always pressure to contrive new objects upon which it can feed and new "metrics" that demonstrate its efficacy, and new terms to sugarcoat the pill.

The Bureaucratic Passive Voice

Executive bureaucratic culture favors the passive voice in communication as a means of depersonalization. When aided by euphemisms and dysphemisms this style of communication can be as subtle or bold as an occasion may require. For a particularly bold example, an annual report of a corporation contained one of the most astonishing euphemisms that I have ever encountered. After the loss of a great deal of money because of disastrous marketing decisions — which went unmentioned in the report — the anonymous corporate writer(s) stated that the corporation had "experienced a period of negative growth."[109]

Note how the use of the characteristically bureaucratic passive voice removes the always-sticky question of responsibility and personal agency, while the term "negative growth" almost sounds as if they planned it. The passive voice depersonalizes ugly, stupid or arbitrary decisions and policies that affect real persons, along with potential culpability for them, decisions that parse up limited resources in ways that may leave many wanting.

A professional interrogator observed to me that the point in a narrative where the voice changes from first person to passive has proven a good indicator to him of possible wrongdoing, e.g., the narrative that contains, "I put the money on top of the safe," becomes at some point, "The money was missing." No actor or agent is to be found in the passive voice version of reality, and therefore no blame. Things just happen.

Another classic example from personal observation: "It has become necessary to close the office for the rest of the afternoon." Here, the Universe itself appears to have conspired to close the office, one might conclude, but not the person who actually shut and locked the door. Political leaders, officials and bureaucrats of all kinds quickly shift into the foggy passive or second person voices when challenged: saying in effect, it's not me — it's circumstances beyond "our" control. Of course when credit can be claimed, personal responsibility quickly returns.

By necessity, depersonalizing and personalizing language pervades modern political speech. Rhetorician Kenneth Burke and sociologist Murray Edelman both noted that a main function of modern mass political language is to sharpen the pointless and blunt the too sharply pointed. Dehumanization and personalization ably serve in both capacities.

Regarding the complementary relationship that often exists between dehumanization and personalization, in the Second World

---

109 Aristotle calls this technique *minimization*. The euphemism, which sees much service in propaganda, is a chief means of minimizing the egregious. The attorney defends the multiple slayer, forger, and thief by saying, "He made a mistake" or "He was a victim of his environment. " The rhetorical reverse of minimization is *amplification*, which, paraphrasing Aristotle, is making one thing seem many. Using amplification, a petty embezzler is reproached: "He stole; he violated his position of trust, the pact of honor that binds all civilized persons; he took knowingly that which was not his." All this is to say but one thing — he couldn't keep his hands out of the till.

War, Stalin allegedly said that ten thousand dead Russian soldiers is a statistic, but a single dead Russian mother's son, a tragedy. Tears of hot grief vivify the mediated portrait of the mother, while "ten thousand casualties" comparatively stands as cold and dry as a sociology lecture. The dehumanized, cold statistic allows for emotional distancing. If the goal is to deeply move the audience, to involve them emotionally, the horror must be shown in personal, human relational terms. This vivification is achieved through personalization, for that is how most people seem to grasp the world. They seem most receptive to crude melodrama. When the goal is to distance a too-real horror, however, the propagandist then chooses the complementary route, the detachment offered by the various means of dehumanization, objectification and euphemisms.

Military censors or media-relations personnel avoid news images that show the caskets of their side in the conflict, especially in quantity, a sight that dramatically signifies the boy or girl in every box. We have all seen caskets with the bodies of our loved ones inside and too well understand viscerally what this means. In the First World War, despite nearly a million United Kingdom military dead, no British newspaper reputedly even showed a photograph of a dead British soldier. Similarly, American news media production managers were loath to show people plummeting from the towers of the World Trade Center.

Such avoidance might seem to contradict the Stalinesque notion of personal tragedy — but actual bodies are perhaps too much. This shocks and reduces *morale*, a term long associated with propaganda and its effects; for good morale is thought vital to successfully sustain a war. A pathos-inducing, grieving mother does not equate with showing autopsy photographs that produce mere horror. People are squeamish. One cannot throw too much in their faces. Propaganda blunts the too-sharply pointed. For these reasons, the personalized *dramaganda* usually just suggests the terrors of death or victimization. The tragedy is seen through the eyes of family and friends, inducing an emotional reaction of manageable size, but well short of a total shock that might be off-putting to audience members.[110] Proper personaliza-

---

110 Behavioral persuasion research back in the 1950s suggested that too strong a fear appeal causes not persuasion, but repression of the message. I don't know how well these findings hold up anymore — for some advertisements are rather horrifying, maybe as an effect of decreasing literacy. Generally, an audience doesn't get it unless it is direct, but brutally direct I am not so sure of.

tion puts human faces and tears on a phenomenon too terrible to face directly, one from which otherwise people would turn away. The drill becomes wedding and graduation photographs of the departed, video footage of the impact on stricken family members and high school chums, a quick edited-in shot of a scrawled message: "We'll miss you, Blinky."

For obvious reasons, the commonly held values of the mass audience force dramatic requirements upon both mass media entertainment and news. Personalization propaganda must address these same values. People seem predisposed to easily absorbable corny packaged stories involving real-seeming people, much more than they are to expository essays that demand thoughtful, conscious work. Personalization and dehumanization provide an easy way for them to grasp things that are otherwise abstract. Even so-called intellectuals are much less "intellectual" in this regard than is commonly supposed. I know this because I work with many. They are as gooey as anyone else in their sentiments, if not more so. Responding to the gooey mass market, news has become less and less "news" in the traditional "objective" sense and more and more dramatized/personalized stories. Reactions of idiots are now routinely broadcast as news. Personalized heroes and villains — not sociology — dominate the popular imagination. A face attached to the phenomenon renders it more immediately knowable.

Thus, the faces of the firemen and emergency response workers became for a time the only available symbolic heroes of 9-11. They were shown with respirators pushed up to reveal grim visages, exhausted but determined, covered in dust, selflessly risking harm. No body parts of victims were shown, though. This was too raw. In such ways, authority banishes disorder, this impression is reinforced by the personal face put on the response: the tireless, duty-bound restorers-of-order. A warm sort of afterglow spread through the land for a while and reflected on local volunteer firefighters, who may have had nothing to do with 9-11, but provided a local face to a distant tragedy.

Even facelessness can become a face, so to speak. Note how films employ the stereotypical, faceless trench-coated minions of fascism, thugs that come at night, the purveyors of the *Nacht und Nebel*, "night and fog." These could be the goose-stepping Nazis of the past, today's cookie-cutter North Korean troops hyper-goose-stepping on review, or the indistinguishable corporate businesspersons in identical blue suits.

A classic example of dehumanization, Frank Capra's previously mentioned 1945 film *Know Your Enemy: Japan* describes Japanese soldiers as being as alike as prints off the same photographic negative. The message: they are not really individuals like us Americans, where the little guy matters, but are instead the worker ants of a demonic horde.

Of course, epithets and metonymy — the latter being a rhetorical device that substitutes a part of something for the whole — also see much use in dehumanization. Metonymy dehumanizes a woman into a cunt, a man into a prick; while epithets turn a black person into a porch monkey, a white person into a pecker-head, *ad infinitum*. There is always a way. On the whole, dehumanization is a necessary prelude to any sort of programmatic abuse.

Michel Foucault shows in his various works how objectifying language, which he daubed the "clinical gaze," has become the basis for many modern power relationships. This is a lexical process of defining problems in such a way as to render them treatable by administrative-bureaucratic means.

For example, the modern educational system sweeps up all matters concerned with imparting knowledge under the mantle of scientism, the religious belief in a science of education, even though one might observe that the rise of modern scientific education colleges has been accompanied by a decline in mass educational standards. This may indicate that propagandizing administrative elites, whose real business is justifying careerism under the fair cloak of scientism, have successfully colonized the educational endeavor. They have dehumanized education, which should perhaps be the most human of all exchanges, with the magical words of pseudoscience. Terms like "pedagogy" and "synergy" are thrown around like their users actually knew what these terms meant. As a means of claiming power, authorities and would-be authorities routinely designate people "at risk," "special needs" and a host of other objectified conditions that beg for treatment and prevention. These terms change over time because authorities must show themselves as progressively scientific — another aspect of the modernist scam. This dehumanization by objectification is necessary because it is obviously immoral to claim power over free persons; but managing a disadvantaged "case," or set of symptoms seems virtually to be a moral obligation. Once again, consider the vague set of misbehaviors called Attention Deficit Disorder that has resulted in the otherwise reprehensible drugging of many thousands — no — millions, of children and young people.

These sorts of dehumanization/personalization techniques also allow the propagandist to play a very strong ethical hand when it suits him (again, see Commandment Eleven on the need for conspicuous displays of ethics and morals in propaganda). Notice how modern American wars help spread something called democratization over less-developed nations in need of such guidance. Vengeance or preemption no longer constitute just cause in this sentimental age. Recall, too, that the era of colonialism was eventually justified with a morality play, the Kiplingesque doctrine of the White Man's Burden, the white man being obliged to help his uncivilized little black and brown brothers by organizing and managing them, like it or not. And as C. S. Lewis observed when comparing modern trends in police work to the sociological mindset, if the cure is good, then how much better is prevention, for there are no limits to prevention.[111]

Personalization or dehumanization are often delivered by means of compelling human-interest stories peopled by martyrs, victims, heroes, caricatures, and stereotypes. It is as easy to write a press release from a human-interest angle as a straight news angle, and often more effective in selling the idea. The impersonal story of welfare reform legislation told as legislative bills, demographics, statistics and trends is seriously boring. Maybe this is how it should be treated if the goal is to disinterest potential voters. However, when personalized via the packaged human-interest news release, welfare reform turns into a tale of hope and triumph wherein the American Dream takes on flesh. Welfare recipient Z is shown getting up at 5 a.m. to pack a poor family's lunch for her children before she takes the long bus ride to the community college to study for a new, hoped-for career as a fashion designer. She is back late at night exhausted, but she perseveres; for she is the "deserving" poor. "How can we measure the worth of a human life?" asks the professional administrators or the politicians who derive their offices on the basis of such programs. And consider the ever popular, "Even if it only saves one life, it's worth it." This personalization

---

111 See Lewis's *That Hideous Strength* (New York: Macmillan, 1946). Lewis, ever the didactic writer whether fictionalizing or not, believed that the older system of punishment was generally more humane because punishment had reasonable limits. But prevention has none and can be used to justify the intervention of authority any time and any place, continually, forever.

conveys the impression that administrators are doing good work, that public money is being well stewarded. Little vignettes such as above, however unrepresentative or misrepresentative, generally take root much better than sociologically-styled studies of workfare programs conducted by think tanks, although the latter have their use too. (See Commandment Ten on the propagandistic need to employ facts, factoids, truth and logic.) Also, who has not seen the ghostwritten (or assisted) biographical and autobiographical bestsellers that instantly crop up concerning any remotely viable political candidate? Such propagandistic memoirs positively personalize, e.g., Bill Clinton's *The Man from Hope,* and Sarah Palin's *Going Rogue.*

I once witnessed a miniature personalization play produced by the directors and employees of a university research center on the occasion of a state legislative committee hearing that was held on campus. The entire hearing was a highly produced, albeit crude, vignette staged for television news and the quick, summative visual, the photo in the newspaper or the one-minute newscast. As these things are done, the timing was early enough in the day so as to be able to meet the production deadlines of the evening news programs. This research center operated a number of human services "demonstration projects" which demonstrated, as far as I could tell, only that it was possible to spend a great deal of money employing social workers on dubious programs alleged to enhance self esteem and personal efficacy of clients, all while providing what amounted to free daycare for them. The programs had so few clients that they were shared and cross-reported by several similar projects in order to build numbers for evaluation purposes.

Local media were invited to the hearings, which consisted of various persons, almost all employed in "paraprofessional" roles by the demonstration projects, who read statements written for them on 3 x 5 inch cards by the programs' principals/social workers. The committee meanwhile sat at a table on an auditorium stage looking officious, which provided yet another good visual. All the while, other employees of the projects chauffeured what few clients and paraprofessionals were to be had back and forth so they could stand up and read more statements that had been written for them. It was utterly contrived and utterly fake. But it did not look that way on the news that night. Those poor people reading the statements looked so pathetically needy. None were identified as employees. Please don't cut our funds, they all said, help the children. The state representatives emanated concern, and were to be seen there on the front lines responding to crisis. The Center had successfully put positive human faces on the program — and funding continued. It still does for all I know.

A vignette, of course, could just as easily have been done with a negative personalization portrayal showing how the sorts of credit cards now issued to welfare recipients see regular use at casinos and Hawaiian resorts.

Personalization treatments may be quite subtle. Others are hatchet jobs. They can be unbelievably petty at times — thus aligning with spiritually small people in general — another reason why the treatments may work so well. Some amount to no more than mean-spirited gossip or rumor, e.g., Bill Clinton's alleged venereal infections. The personalization treatment may come to represent the problem, often employing what people commonly refer to as "stereotypes." News media personalization treatments quite often show rather clearly the political-social bias that may be inherent in news organization personnel. Look at coverage of the so-called Tea Party recently where reporters somehow manage to interview the least sympathetic person(s) among hundreds. (Reporters, too, are professionally interested in personalization drama — as this is a general news value that sells news by making stories that are of interest to more people.) Human-interest stories tainted by negative personalization treatment may become dark psychological profiles speculating in unwholesome motivations such as paranoia or physical inadequacy. Some of this is due no doubt to the shared cultural values of elites who generate news agendas and create news treatments, e.g., the NPR crowd.

Even the photographs selected by news media and interest groups for use in stories may be carefully culled for the most flattering or unflattering shot, depending on the desired effect. Classic negative treatments — one sees these all the time — select shots of people with mouths open, grimacing, unaware or in attitudes of surprise or awkwardness. The positive shot shows people smiling, poised, surrounded by family members or other wholesome persons, e.g., the law enforcement leaders or children that the handlers of Presidents Obama or Clinton assembled for pseudo-events staged at the White House.

The propagandist, whether acting to promote or demote, always strives to find that perfect poster child to symbolize the cause. Even when engineering a key test case before the U.S. Supreme Court, advocacy groups will shop for the plaintiff that best personalizes the issue.

Some cases and plaintiffs are simply more sympathetic than others. This is why, for example, *McDonald v. Chicago*, the recent gun rights case that resulted in the incorporation of the Second Amendment under the Fourteenth Amendment, hinged upon the attractive personality of Otis McDonald, an older black man who wanted a gun for self defense. There were plenty of white men in Chicago, to be sure, in the same position, but they were less sympathetic at first glance — which is the only glance the propagandist usually gets from any audience. Gun rights advocates obviously wished to counteract the prevalent television-derived stereotype of the white male gun owner.

The celebrity spokesperson is of course an extreme personalization. The cute, little gecko whose personality unfolds through a series of automobile insurance advertisements is perhaps even more effective. Such a personable but imaginary spokes-personality has the advantage of being totally manageable. There is no chance of the gecko driving his car into a tree or being involved in a messy divorce that may come to be associated with the product to which his image is attached — unless of course the writers wish to introduce such antics for the sake of novelty.

Also widespread in personalization propaganda, depending on conditions, it may often be useful to put a face on the enemy so that a conflict can be understood in human terms. At the same time, the propagandist dehumanizes the enemy masses so that it becomes easier to kill them. Hitler proved an ideal subject for negative personalization treatments and caricature. The toothbrush mustache, the uniforms, the extreme gesticulations, the guttural, comic sounds of the German language — all proved irresistible material for mockery by allied propagandists and entertainers. Hitler was attributed with all sorts of negative personal traits. Beyond the rumors and songs attributing him just one testicle, cartoons ridiculed him as the little corporal dressed up as a great man.

Of course the Germans held him up for reverence as a father figure, hero and economic savior. There is no mistaking the authenticity of the benign reception he received from the crowds, women and children included, as shown in Leni Riefenstahl's great propaganda film *Triumph of the Will*. Here, Hitler moves among the crowds with virtually no security or military presence, a feat no modern American president could safely attempt. At the same time, propaganda filmmakers like Frank Capra allowed the Nazis to dehumanize themselves — they simply cut bits of marchers from the Nazi's own films, re-contextualized them, added voiceovers, and showed the Nazis as inhuman automatons or clowns. For the latter see the Dancing Nazi Ballet film, which delighted British and American audiences by using clever editing (for 1942) to make Nazi marchers appear to dance chorus-girl-style to the mindless, popular tune called the Lambeth Walk.

An extreme modern example, current "Green" propaganda for carbon emissions public service advertisements suggests it is acceptable to kill the non-compliant literally by exploding them. By their own piggish acts they have lost their right to live communally and are on the instant reduced to bloody gobs of tissue splattered about in classrooms and workplaces. Eco-fascism anyone?

Politicians, products much like any others, are invariably anthropomorphized by their handlers and supporters. In my view, this not only misrepresents them, but contributes to serious intellectual mistakes in understanding their actions. Most I have met seem more like creatures of base instincts than paragons of virtue. Politicians are typically shown in posed events mingling with the people, sometimes in shirtsleeves to show that they are just "regular" folk. In these vignettes they are sometimes surrounded with their own and other people's more presentable children and spouses. We hear stories of fortitude, hardships and triumphs designed to put a likeable human face on a performance that otherwise might be interpreted less charitably as a mindless groping for power. The message of course: he/she worked his way up; he/she eats simple food; he/she is a regular fellow just like you and me, *simpatico*. The epithet can be handy here as well e.g., "The Great Communicator." Conversely, one could dehumanize a politician by labeling him or her as part of a political machine, or personalize via a darker sort of epithet, e.g., "Tricky Dick" or "The Governator." All these practices are routine and almost automatic.

Dictated by circumstances, for propaganda works with the tools and situations available, one needs to put a face on it — or remove the face, or substitute a stereotype for it, especially if one intends to kill it.

The Tenth Commandment

DISPENSE TRUTH, FACTS, LOGIC AND SCIENCE

In this age of fact worshippers, "Show me the evidence" is a demand made even by children. Virtually everybody thinks himself the critical thinker, the analyst, as smart if not smarter than others, gifted with discernment. A paradigm of scientific, measurable hard-nosed realism reigns. Even the avowedly religious call first on medical science and then on God, and as judged by popular culture there seems little doubt which one is currently the prestige paradigm.

The scientistic situation, scientism being defined as a naively absolutist religious- like belief in science, has actually simplified the work of propagandists considerably, because it in effect has created a higher absolute reality from which there can be no easy and ready common-sense appeal, and certainly none based on mere faith or the old virtues. This higher reality is forever being discovered and improved upon, this meta-world of unimpeachable scientific factuality. Of course people make of science a lot more than it really has to offer concerning ultimate explanations, or even mundane ones. We have yet to see a satisfactory scientific explanation of the phenomenon of an enjoyable dinner with old and tested friends, or a good book, or for that matter a fine afternoon? Such are contemporary expectations, however, that a college student once asked in my presence when a discussion of the origin of the universe came up, "Why don't we just ask a computer?" Science has replaced Magic, with Religion relegated to a bit of space at the back of the broom storage closet, to be called upon only when there is a really big mess to clean up.

The popular expectation is that Science, however childishly conceived, will tell us what was, is and shall be, which used to be Religion's job. Science will save us. It has, in fact, delivered in innumerable ways and thereby improved the common lot and standard of living — e.g., trauma repair, agriculture and engineering. But where the conscientious, prudent scientist fears to tread, or only goes with highly specified trepidations, propagandists rush in and thrive by scientistically explaining the world in ways that benefit their organizations or causes.

Anything even vaguely scientific will often do in the way of explanation or justification. Eight out of ten doctors say that you should buy this remedy. A random survey finds an association between longevity and exercise. A study published in a medical journal shows gun owners at higher risk of homicide than non-gun owners. A PowerPoint slide, one of 60 or so in what consultants call "a deck" used for a presentation, graphs student retention, projected upward, of course, as the result of the new administrative initiative. There you have it. Science. Propaganda is positively adrip with science. And this is good enough for many. People talk about "junk science" and "pseudoscience," but usually in dismissing ideas with which they disagree. How can you fight science save with more and better science? Even Creationist fundamentalists now counterattack Evolutionist scientists with scientists of their own.

Anyone who has ever taken a research methodology class dealing with causes and effects knows that scientific conclusions are more rightly referred to as inferences, especially so in the social and behavioral sciences, where it is often next to impossible to isolate experimental conditions from the influence of confounding variables.[112] Such causal inferences are usually quite limited and highly conditional, subject to all sorts of measurement validity and reliability

---

112 Reality is the biggest confounding variable of them all.

checks, in addition to the challenges to validity of inferences posed by a host of internal and external experimental conditions. Above and beyond all this, basic statistical assumptions need to be satisfied. To understand such limitations one has to actually learn the methodologies and read the studies, daunting tasks considering the methodological and linguistic armor in which such studies tend to be written, made even more so by the relative obscurity of the specialized, professional and academic journals in which they tend to appear. Personally, I am unconvinced that most professors, who stand among the chief promulgators of such empirical knowledge, even read the journals in their fields. The ones in communication, for example, are generally as unreadable as they are uninteresting — although many professors subscribe and display journal issues on their office bookshelves, it is unclear whether this is to convince themselves or visitors of their expertise.[113] So-called normal people who lack time, energy, interest and resources to do their own scientific investigating, generally must rely on interpreters, informational middlemen, who just happen to be journalists and propagandists. Journalists, of course, get most of their official information from the propagandists. Usually, when one hears about a scientific finding it is because some PR functionary working for the organization that generated the finding wrote a press release or made a video feed for television news.

Also, when one attempts to apply them generally, scientific findings are often half-truths, or quarter-truths, or less, owing to the conditions imposed by research designs. Taken from their artificial context, they may collapse.

Another factor that enhances the power of scientistic propaganda is the absurd proposition that rationality governs human conduct. Whether people are rational decision-makers or after-the-fact rationalizers of actions is always a good question. Astute propagandists would say that people find rational explanations for the things they have already done or believed. The psychoanalysts and behavioral psychologists have long known, after a century plus of research and case studies that people tend to be rationalizing more than rational animals.

---

113 The main ostensible purpose of these peer reviewed scholarly journals is the dissemination of research or new knowledge. The main de facto purpose, however, at least in most cases, seems to be tenure and promotion. Don't get me wrong here. I am all for the tenure of qualified people, as it is the only thing that protects real scholarship from administration's excesses and self-justificatory whims, but there are many frauds and poseurs.

In the opinion of Henry Adams, grandson of the American President Adams, people resorted to reason only for lack of proper training.[114] On the whole, people resort to reason to make virtue out of necessity, for sour-grape explanations, for explanations concerning the nature of the world and their low or afflicted places in it, and for an uncountable multitude of ego defense purposes. People need and seek reasons for the thing(s) they have already become, or done, or wish to do, or cannot do, and they may often find them in propaganda, the purveyors of which are always willing to oblige in this manner, providing it suits the overall purposes of the propaganda. It is well known that people will seek out technical and consumer information on big-ticket items like cars after, and not before, they have purchased the item. Technical facts explain behavior; they do not necessarily determine it. A 60-year-old man does not buy a red sports car because of its overhead cams, however wonderful those may be. Classic examples from behavioral persuasion research include what are called *cognitive dissonance, equilibrium* and *consistency* theories that posit attitude change (expressed opinions) as a way to rationalize prior behaviors. For example, if a person is maneuvered into a public commitment, even a small one, attitude change in the direction suggested by the action follows, for one must rationally explain behaviors to oneself and others.[115] As a rule, facts don't guide decisions or actions, but justify ones already made. This is true at both the organizational and individual level.[116]

Accordingly, propagandists churn out truth, facts, data, information, studies, evaluations, expertise, assessments, statistics, surveys, documentaries, reports and logical arguments based on another well-verified principle in propaganda: that a torrent of information drowns a person more than it informs him in any meaningful sense. Much modern public relations work consists of collecting and

---

114 See his whiney but witty intellectual autobiography *The Education of Henry Adams*, editions of which are now available free online.

115 This, again, was the thinking behind Communist indoctrination where one made public confessions and social criticisms, e.g., American prisoners in the Korean War were encouraged to write and read essays critical of American social conditions to their fellow prisoners and captors. In return they received food, but also a subtle shift in attitude that was more conducive to the critical revolutionary state of mind.

116 Another interesting finding of persuasion research is that people will generally let someone cut in line or commit some other transgression if that someone first gives a reason — even though the reason may be a *non sequitur*.

providing "facts," albeit carefully sieved, for backgrounders, press kits, press releases and websites. Some approaches to advertising are built on more or less salient factuality, e.g., the David Ogilvy advertising approach, although his approach preceded him.[117] Who can assess a thousand facts, or factoids, of dubious or obscure origins? This takes a focused effort far beyond the individual norm and usually requires an organizational response. As far as the individual goes, as Jacques Ellul points out, myriad facts just leave behind a vague general impression: "Oh yeah, that global warming is a big problem."

Yet another major factor empowers scientistic propaganda. People typically think of propaganda as lies. This vapid misconception facilitates the work of the propagandist, for nothing could be further from the truth than to say that propaganda is lies. Because they are expecting propaganda to stink of whopping lies, or base emotional appeals, they do not associate overwhelming factuality with propaganda. Although the propagandist can, and does, use many carefully selected truths to create a big lie, or a small one if that will suffice, the really big assertions or beliefs of propaganda concern the interpretation of the meaning of data, of evidence and of facts — and these, strictly speaking, lie beyond the cold facts and comprise instead what Aristotle called artistic persuasion, which is much akin to connecting the dots to draw a picture, each dot being, of course, a factual piece of evidence. What the propagandist does not tell is that there may be a whole lot of ways of connecting the dots for any given set of facts. On the whole, propaganda is truthful, albeit selectively truthful. Propagandists equivocate. They tendentiously select and define, when they bother to define at all, for it is almost always better to let the audience member project his own mental preconceptions into the mix, e.g., the meaning of "change." They ignore that which is inconvenient to their purposes, unless it cannot be ignored, in which case they attack it with other facts. A basic assumption of modern American public relations and education is that if given the right information, people will make the right choice. PR people most definitely give it to them in volley fire. All the facts they can eat.

Administrators who run things often have an attitude toward facts and logic as follows. Intellectual workers are mere menials who shovel ideas. One can always hire sociologists or statisticians. The graduate

117 *Ogilvy on Advertising* (New York: Vintage 1985).

schools extrude them in quantity. Additionally, doctoral programs produce as an unfortunate byproduct many half-formed PhDs, who are often called "ABDs" for "All But Dissertation." These people are available for use as data gnomes and can he hired to collect and horde facts, run statistical regressions and multivariate analyses, conduct survey interviews, whatever. Administrators are careful not to overpay them. If there are data to mine, the data gnomes will mine them in the twilight of social science research centers. They are not even unionized.

Administrators have no particular respect for the inherent content — just for looks and effects. One data set or study is as good as another if it gets the job done, plugs the hole in the line, provides a justification, shows a need for services or provides a positive program assessment. Scholarship and research become sandbags in a levee. Pile it on. Another bag needed here. There is no essential regard for the ideas themselves, or the people who live the ideas. Ideas are only as good as they are useful. Administrators are pragmatic, as is propaganda, which is why Barbara Tuchman called propaganda "an unhappy necessity."[118] Propinquity rules.

The Consultant Game

Calling in outside consulting experts to justify administrative programs is a favorite technique of those who make their livings by spending other people's money. The more money spent, the better the consultant, by pecuniary definition. A consultant is a voice from the heavens, so to speak, who presumably has the advantage of a clear eye and wisdom unbiased by infra-organizational politics and interests. In practice, consultants tend to offer limited ranges of services along very predictable lines of expertise. They are known quantities, so with a bit of shopping, administrators know reasonably well what they are getting in advance of whatever report is offered, and before any contract is signed with the consultant. Sometimes the consultant's report may be delivered in the form of a PowerPoint presentation as the only

---

118 A phrase she used in discussing the irrecoverable world public opinion/propaganda blunders that Germany made in the course of trampling Belgian neutrality in 1914. Barbara W. Tuchman, *The Guns of August* (New York: Macmillan Company, 1962), p. 322.

tangible, if one might use this word, product of the consultation. If a consultant's work is somehow not useful to administrators, it is buried or ignored, and another hired. The advantage accrued to administration by the use of consultants is the credibility gained by a difficult-to-refute legitimizing claim of scientifically expert managerial prowess from above. It can be used to justify hard, head-rolling actions, downsizing, reorganization, creation of new programs, ventures, whatever is desired. The Oracle of Science has spoken as it has been paid to do. Administrators may also cherry pick through consultant advice, tendentiously choosing, or simply keep changing consultants until they get what they want. It's also a good way to hire buddies. Consultants provide a higher legitimacy for interior decisions and mitigate the blame factor: as in, "It wasn't us, it was the consultant's report." Science demanded it.

Subpropaganda and Prepropaganda

A planned propaganda campaign often begins with laying the groundwork well in advance of the main thrust. If the overall long-term plan is to promote new environmental regulations, let's say, then subpropaganda, like sub-flooring, is laid first by creating or resurrecting scientific information and releasing it into appropriate media channels. These channels would include education and scientific journals. Reports and projects on threatened species, or airborne emissions, urban farming, or contamination levels are funded, created and disseminated. Some call this *consciousness raising* or *raising awareness*. For example, public health style research on the unintended consequences of defensive gun ownership that alleged owning a gun was a risk factor in homicide, and dissemination of this research via mass media channels, preceded legislative agendas on gun control and attempts to limit guns as public health hazards via governmental regulatory agencies. The current lead hazard scare seems similar in intent. Much, if not most, funded research is purposive in similar ways. Accidental findings do not generally appear in media. Information serves a purpose; it does not appear spontaneously.

The research game, as with consulting, is often rigged so that the RFPs (Request for Proposals) from funding agencies stipulate exactly what sort of research is desired. If the proposals received do not reflect that purpose — the RFP is generally *very* specific — they are not favorably reviewed or funded. Federal and state grants are sometimes "wired," meaning that the RFP is written in such a way as to assure it will go to a pre-selected organization that will deliver just the sort of intellectual-scientific work needed. The reason that think tanks, policy wonks and other associations cluster on the Washington Beltway is partly because policy makers, government and private associations, have created a centralized, sponsored market that patronizes justificatory scientistic research. Additionally, a common conclusion of research reports is that more research needs to be done. The system perpetuates itself.

Op-ed pieces offer another common way of introducing scientistic subpropaganda. In the 1990s while conducting a content analysis of elite newspaper coverage of interest groups, I came across an opinion piece in the prestigious *New York Times* that philosophically investigated whether it was time for civil rights organizations to abandon their policy of integration and move on to more of a separatist approach in education that pedagogically promised better results for black youth. The annual NAACP convention was scheduled a week or two after. One of the themes of the convention was this very same question. A coincidence? Of course not! Opinion leaders (more accurately, their PR people and ghostwriters) routinely use similar means, placing ghostwritten op-ed, "thought" pieces in prominent media. They are much-used in political analysis, in pushing or defusing agendas, where trends and facts — once again used as dots connected to form a picture envisioned by some alleged political expert — are used to demonstrate some desired or undesirable version of reality. Also muchused in creating a saturated atmosphere of factuality are special and investigative committees and their bulky reports that almost no one reads, but which inform press releases and, therefore, news reports. Also ubiquitous is the poll or survey that does "need-assessment" for social services or political programs, e.g., 67 percent of Americans want better health care services. "We will oblige them," declaims the health care administrator or politician, who just happens to have on hand a 2,000-page copy of proposed legislation drawn up by consultants and research centers.

Academics, professors and scientists have proven extremely pliable to the needs of propagandists. A bit of research funding, social advancement or celebrity (or sometimes just gaining prestige in peer group opinion) is often all it takes to seduce them to the cause. I will note a few cases. In 1914, a group of 93 prominent German scientists and academics signed a letter defending the Kaiser's violation of Belgian neutrality when Germany sent its armies through Belgium in a long-planned enveloping move of the French army and the British Expeditionary Force. The Germans, outraged that even civilians shot at them (which they regarded as uncivilized), took and killed thousands of hostages, men and women, burned out entire towns, and then were further upset, indignant even, when people in the occupied zones disliked them afterward. They also claimed that Belgian women were poking out the eyes of wounded German soldiers. The letter testified to the civilizing effects of German culture.

In Soviet Russia, it was so important that the science of biology agree with official Marxist–Leninist Political Philosophy, that the government created a scientific school of thought now known as Lysenkoism, in which scientists sought and found evidence for what is called Lamarckian evolution. Although discredited in the West as the basic evolutionary mechanism, Lamarckian evolution better aligns with the Marxist historical tenet that social evolution occurs through revolutionary class warfare. Marxism itself is a highly scientized view of social history, hence a perfect propaganda aimed at people who regard themselves as intellectuals of some sort, wherein history is seen as subject to alleged "laws" of dialectical economic determinism, and thus will inevitably arrive at Communism. The Marxist state could not therefore tolerate the idea that random mutation drove natural selection, i.e., Darwin's mechanism of evolution, a mechanism that might lead elsewhere and anywhere other than Communism.[119]

The current global warming scare exhibits many signs of "cooked" science. The many television commercials employing it as a premise may be a giveaway. It's too trendy. Elders may recall that forty years ago scientists were predicting a global winter as result of air pollution. Today it is global summer. Having little idea of where the truth lies in this matter, a healthy skepticism may be advisable regarding any science that advances administrative truth and careers as heavy-handedly

---

119 The Lamarckian idea was that evolution resulted from each generation attempting something beyond its present abilities. So let's say that each generation stretched to reach for high-hanging fruit, or to better play long intervals on the piano, then future generations would develop longer more supple fingers. This notion of revolutionary selection fitted the idea of historical class struggle. Lysenkoist state-funded scientists in the old U.S.S.R. even provided supporting physical scientific evidence.

as global warming scientism. Its direct implication is regulatory necessity: continued and more administration will save us, the universal modern message of propaganda.

Bureaucratic Logic, Truth and Beauty

As a child I thought that many adults I came across in institutional settings were stupid. They seemed obvious liars, too, propounding ridiculous, logical explanations for why I should do what they wanted when it seemed plain that the battle was for domination and nothing more. When I became an adult, I learned that the situation was really much worse than I had originally imagined.

In organizational life, logic similarly becomes a tool of domination. Organizational logic, the bounded logic of the professions, the quasi-professions (e.g., teaching) and bureaucratic functionalism, exist perhaps as the only consistent logical framework that many people ever know.

The organizational world is a world of power and lack of power. Some have power. Some don't. Many want it. Few wish to share it. Just a smidgen of power produces a sort of madness, a species of bloated gloating. See what happens when even the most minor bureaucrat is challenged, e.g., a child questioning a teacher, or a faculty governance body questioning a university president. A challenge, even if indirect, assures a willful, negative response: "See what I can do to you. How do you like it?" is the message, although expressed in terms of objective process and procedure, e.g., grades and rewards or budgets and reorganizations. When bureaucrats say they want input, this generally means they want subordinates to conform to the party line. Discussion is intended to achieve conformity.

A major purpose of any bureaucracy is to say "no" and confine the disbursements of scarce resources in such a manner that can be defended as objective and impersonal, when they may well be everything but. There is only so much of the good stuff to go around, and the bureaucracy must defend the current distribution and future allocations. To test this proposition, go down and see how business is conducted at the local county courthouse.

The whole modern administrative enterprise is founded and legitimized on a premise of scientific, rational thought. Bureaucracy is synonymous with modern scientific organization. The premise remains as a legitimating claim even if organization should serve irrational and unscientific ends, e.g., fat cat administrators and self-perpetuating functionaries who operate at general social expense. The problem of justification is always inherent in scientific rational organization, hence their prominent use of mission or vision statements as ethical goals (see Commandment Eleven on the need to demonstrate ethics). Controlling the flow of information (Commandment One) also conveys great advantages when it comes to justifying bureaucracy.

Also from the propagandistic perspective, what rational bureaucracies do well is depersonalize (Commandment Nine) their often highly personal decisions concerning who gets what, when and how. This makes decisions seem less political or arbitrary.[120] Sorry, you can't have that because it belongs to the organization, one is told; or regulatory protocol requires process X to be implemented. Despite all this, however, cronies, friends and relatives often manage to benefit. Again, a major purpose of the bureaucracy is saying no, while affirming the privileges of the right sort of interior people and cliques.

Those excluded are consoled with a letter, often a form letter, saying, in effect, and often in a passive voice, that there were so many applicants who were so well qualified, that even though it was a difficult decision you had to be passed by. A recruiting manager I know calls this genre of communication, examples of which are modeled in many business communication textbooks, the "fuck-you-very-much letter." They are sometimes exquisitely phrased, especially when written by master propagandists. I saw one from the White House once that was so complimentary it had to be read very carefully to realize that it fits the genre just mentioned.

The Assessment and Evaluation Game

Self-serving, quantitative program evaluations have been elevated to a modern art form, the assessment being a fetish that comes to substitute for performance. I witnessed once the assembly of a program evaluation for a project designed to reduce the drop out rate of black

---

120 See Harold Lasswell's book on politics, called, appropriately enough, *Politics: Who Gets What, When, Where, How* (Whittlesy House: London, 1935).

males from a set of urban high schools, a proportion that exceeded 50 percent both before and after the program.

The program was usual enough on the surface. It was funded by a well-known foundation, which had insisted on a formal evaluation as part of its standard grant-making practices. In partnership with the local school system, the program consisted in part of "enrichment activities" provided by university educators such as film attendance and cultural events. Also included were mentoring and group activities including special classes and social outings to movies. By the end of year one, almost all of the original target population of black males had dropped out. In order to fill space in the program, its staff added more students, but since black males were not generally available, they accepted female students. As the program wound down to its conclusion in year three, virtually all the students were black females. A successful evaluation was impossible if one looked at the retention rates of the target population, which approached zero. Instead, the program evaluators used measures such as client satisfaction indexes, where 90 percent, or so, of program participants reported on a survey "instrument" developed by the program, that they had enjoyed the rides on the bus and other activities such as the films. This was called a high success rate while the fact that the subjects evaluated were in nowise the same subjects who had begun the program was conveniently ignored.

Mumbo Jumbo, Magical Thinking and Cargo Cult Education

How many people really understand everyday mechanical technologies, which are merely straightforward applications of scientific principles, let alone the more complicated theories that purportedly reveal the inner workings of cellular biology or subatomic physics? Most people don't even understand how a toilet works, let alone a computer. As far as functional-level understanding goes, such items may as well be magical boxes. When critics ridicule economic theories and political claims by calling them "voodoo economics" they are making a valid point. Who really understands? What does the mumbo jumbo mean, guns and butter, economic indices, recessions, quantitative easing, and so on? If economists knew so much about economics, then why aren't they all rich?[121]

Much supposedly modern scientific thinking strongly resembles primitive magical thinking. Magical words and rituals promise the sort of control over reality that defines power — so do medical and scientific vocabularies. Historically, whether magic and magical words worked for achieving any supernatural effects on behalf of the practitioners and their patrons I cannot say. They obviously worked very well, though, in helping practitioners, or their patrons, obtain earthly social power over their fellow men. Magicians and priests, sometimes in hereditary orders that lasted hundreds or thousands of years, have held great power, either directly or by advising and consecrating rulers — e.g. ancient Egypt's theocracies, Rome's priests and vestal virgins, the Pope's traditional anointing of kings and emperors, or the monk Rasputin's reputedly unsavory hold over the Russian Royal Family.

In much the same way, more modern "brain trusts" of experts, organized into professional and academic orders, are called upon to inform the policies of the leaders who are their patrons, e.g., presidential cabinets. Whereas the ancients read omens and auguries such as chicken entrails and the flights of birds, today's social scientific experts interpret public opinion, economic trends, agricultural and military reports and other intelligence, hoping to render a public policy convincingly fortified by Science. Either process may be equally mysterious.

Ritualized science pervades education, popular and organizational cultures. Scientific thinking degenerates into mindless incantations dealing with the breakthroughs and innovations, trends and buzzwords, such as social media, network marketing, transformative change, dietary fiber, strategic planning, distance learning. In addition to heavy use in advertising, ritualized quasi-science lends bulk, if not substance, to many corporate undertakings. Higher education turns toward scientism as a consequence of having been refocused for the mass market, education being no longer a process of dialectic and a guided, often painstaking, interior development, but instead

---

121 Francis Bacon made the same point about fortune tellers and magicians. If they knew so much about the inner workings of the universe, then why are they so often desperate, powerless and poor? And why do magic and the supernatural find such a warm welcome in the lowest most desperate classes? Economists are perhaps the modern equivalent.

a technologically modern assembly line that injection-molds "outcomes" using the latest standardized materials and applications — e.g., distance learning modules.

The mass higher education approach especially resembles the *cargo cult*, a quasi-religious social phenomenon that occurs when technologically developed powers have rolled over undeveloped primitive cultures. In New Guinea, for example, virtually stone-age natives saw for the first time western technological paraphernalia, which they understood only as a markedly improved form of magic. Giant silver birds, airplanes, would deliver rich cargo to the Europeans: jeeps, rifles and other obviously magical devices. These indigenous peoples, quite sensibly, stopped working at the traditional pursuits and beliefs that had sustained them and focused on adapting the new brand of magic, borrowing both Western millenarian religious and administrative ritualized behaviors. Cults sprang up: a messianic god-savior in the volcano would send giant silver birds to the natives, loaded with cargo. Using sympathetic magic, natives constructed administrative compounds of sticks, where dressed in cast-off western clothing they went through the motions of office work and typing. Imitation airstrips were cleared around airplane effigies to encourage the silver birds to land. Rather than into sensible work, energy was drained into these rituals.[122]

A great deal of this kind of behavior takes place in modern universities, education colleges and high schools. Here students expect to memorize a list of magical words or procedures, receive a review sheet, recognize the words on the multiple choice test, and otherwise go through the motions so they can realize the implied promise of cargo — the good job and life that result from "education," which is essentially having money, that most magical of things. Application, creative work and understanding don't figure in. Incantation is the thing, rather than a longish, somewhat hazy developmental process. Educational administrators can't resist the temptation of the cargo cult — and may not themselves know the difference between work and ritual. Neither can demagogues who would educate by decree. They steer the curriculum toward the market. The less-flashy business of true education that requires effective, subtle developmental work cannot compete with cargo cult mass education.

---

122 See V. Lanternari's *Religions of the Oppressed* (New York: A.A. Knopf, 1963).

Mass politics would not be possible without magical thinking disguised as science and logic, e.g., new shibboleth-like solutions, the technological-scientific miracles, new alternative sources of energy and the "green" economics of farming the burned out acreage in decayed cities that will provide new green food sources.

Probably the most common propagandistic logic of the political world is the deductive syllogism[123] based on uncertain or false premises: "Government spending stimulates the economy to create prosperity; the government will stimulate the economy by spending; therefore the United States will be prosperous." While it may sometimes be true that this happens, and government spending certainly benefits those who get it and those who manage the money, prosperity never seemed to have happened as a result of the considerable spending of the Great Depression, which only World War II appears to have ended. At best the truth or falsity of the premise is uncertain, like so many other propositions in the social-political sphere, but yet such logic is often accepted at face value. Here's another: "More money spent on mass education equals better education for each student," a premise that administrators love.

As we are so often in the fog, causality often consisting of intelligent guesswork, the propagandist provides simple logic that interprets the situation favorably for him, projecting an image unto the fog of events, and people, thus cued, then imagine it is actually there. The suggestibility of people is enormous in this regard.

Few have the training, time, energy or degree of burning involvement (and paradoxically, some degree of intellectual detachment) prerequisite to mine through such material on their own, even under the best of circumstances. Bathe them in the superstitious glow of factuality, technology, science, and logic and they will be overwhelmed.

---

123 Please pardon the tautology, but all syllogisms are deductive. I do this merely for emphasis. As Aristotle explained, there are only two ways to prove anything: (1) through examples, inductions, that build up to a general conclusion, and (2) syllogisms, or deductive arguments that take a generally known truth (or belief) and apply it to a specific situation. This is why I so strongly recommend reading Aristotle and also why people still read him 2000 plus years later.

The Eleventh Commandment

DEMONSTRATE GOOD ETHICS (AND DON'T GET CAUGHT)

A s far as propagandists and their employers are concerned, good propaganda is effective propaganda — and to be effective, propaganda must appear ethical. Ethics are practiced virtues, although in politics and administrative life ethics are often merely referred to in a sweeping way, or used as assurance or justification for real or proposed actions, e.g., a code of ethics or a vision statement deflects criticism by functioning much like a protective screen for manifold administrative efforts.

Name-Game Ethics

Administrative need drives meaning. In modern American, colloquial English the word "propaganda" is a pejorative. In English as spoken perhaps two hundred years ago, however, the term was a narrowly defined noun. As mentioned early in this book, a person referred to as a "propagandist" would likely have been assumed to be a Jesuit, a label with many negative (or at least ambivalent) connotations owing to the political intrigues and tricky logic attributed to the Jesuits, but the term had no other meaningful context. By around the First World War in 1914, however, the term propaganda had been assigned a broad secular meaning by political authorities and was mainly associated with deceptive claims of a decidedly non-ethical sort, especially in wartime contexts, and always by a despised enemy, whomever that happened to be.

A triumph of British and American propaganda during the twentieth century was the successful attachment, in the popular mind, of the label of "propaganda" to Germany, both in the First and Second World Wars, and also, later, to Japan, the Soviet Union and to dictatorships and totalitarianism in general. To many people propaganda will forever be Joseph Goebbels, Tokyo Rose and International Communism, but it was the British and later the Americans who were best at propaganda — don't forget they won. The Germans were klutzy when dealing out propaganda (and diplomacy) outside their own borders, never apparently understanding that what they regarded as expediency, others viewed as moral outrage. Being so comparatively forthright about propaganda, they never did seem to understand that having a "Minister of Propaganda" did them no good on the international scene. Americans disguised their efforts under labels such as the Committee of Public Information and, later on in World War II, the Office of Wartime Information and also at times under the U.S. Army Signal Corps, which released some classic propaganda films. Even American mass entertainment was entrained to propaganda. This effort met with dazzling popular success in the World War II era with its Popeye v. Tojo cartoons, Three Stooges parodies of Hitler and popular singer Kate Smith's sales of war bonds and vigorous belting out of hit songs such as "Praise the Lord and Pass the Ammunition."

In so many ways the Nazis and their vaunted propaganda were amateurish compared to the British and the Americans, e.g., the Nazi attempt to harness P. G. Wodehouse, the creator of the Jeeves series of comic novels, to German propaganda. Nowadays when one says "propaganda" people quickly think of jackboots and swastikas, a direct result of these Anglo-American efforts, but in modern America people might do better to think of the brittle-looking plastic Barbie women and Ken men who staff so many contemporary PR jobs that provide the information that knits together the modern world.

The dark, popular connotations, however, explain why today's propagandists, although legion, will neither call themselves nor admit to being "propagandists." This unstated taboo even seems in many cases to extend to their rationalizations concerning their own careers, a matter of little apparent scruple to many. Some are no doubt simple, as might be expected from lower-level technicians and functionaries, but many, especially at the higher levels, presumably should know better.

Maybe this situation should be considered an example of how the well-educated tend to be more, not less, susceptible to propaganda owing to their commitment to a world of symbols and ideas. They explain the world to suit their own interests. Since "education" so often appears as a synonym for "propaganda," such overall results should not surprise.

People educated in PR believe their own PR. PR professionals protest, overly much it seems, when confronted with the propagandist label, claiming that propaganda and public relations are fundamentally different. College textbooks defend this proposition with elaborate defenses of how "ethical", "transactive" and "two-way" PR practice allegedly may be; and how PR professionals must be included in the very highest circles of organizational leaders, an idea that descends from the Nazi era, where they may best interpret the needs of the public to the organization, and the needs of the organization to the public.

While this sort of talk represents first rate ethical posturing, constituting an exemplary use of ethics in the making of propaganda, it is not at all the same thing as an ethic actually based on true communication. Communication in PR equates with domination, not communion, save in name.[124] Manipulating a target audience, learning its vulnerabilities and grid coordinates, obtaining "feedback" to improve message penetration, is not at all the same thing as a conversation between equals. From the point of view of the target audience, the situation is more like talking to the police without a lawyer: what you say *will* indeed be used against you.

Looking at origins, a good way to understand any phenomenon, Edward Bernays used the terms propaganda and public relations

---

124 Propaganda scholar J.M. Sproule, for one, disapproves of the "communication as domination paradigm" that has driven a great portion of the academic study of communication during the past 75 years or so.

virtually interchangeably. Further, he made no secret of how his work in "public information" for the propaganda organization formed by President Wilson to mobilize the public to support American involvement in World War I, the Committee on Public Information (CPI), suggested to him the commercial business of public relations that he pursued so fruitfully after the War. CPI is generally acknowledged as an archetype of modern propaganda machinery, and Bernays as the somewhat quirky Father of Public Relations.

Bernays later joked about "proper-ganda" and "improper-ganda," saying that CPI made the proper sort. The "proper-gandist" of these days is often trained as a PR person. The self-avowed propagandist, however, is possibly more honest with himself and others than one disguised as a public relations professional. This is not to cast doubt on the professionalism of PR people; it is just a question of the realm in which to properly assign their activities. Bernays also asserted, based on good evidence, that it was propaganda that had made American uniquely great — creating markets and expanding the nation, lubricating the thrust of modernity so to speak. Despite colloquial, connotative meanings, neither *propaganda* nor *public relations* are necessarily negative terms. Another common and rather thin ethical defense is that PR/propaganda subsidize and otherwise make available information that would not otherwise have been available, thereby allowing people more options in making choices. How this differs from pandering remains unclear.

Propagandists would agree indeed, e.g., Bernays and Goebbels, that PR/propaganda expertise belongs at the highest levels of any organization to assure success. Hitler, who started out in the Nazi party as its propagandist, dictated a chapter in his book *Mein Kampf* to describing the vital role of propaganda in the growth of the successful political movement. PR expertise (but not necessarily formal training) has also been identified as a key to success in climbing the corporate organizational ladder — PR used here in the sense of deftness in blame-dodging and credit-taking.[125] Modern administration depends on propaganda, which may in many instances represent its most significant work product, e.g., the gypsy university provost who moves from one set of imaginary triumphs, as represented by programs of no substance or follow-through as listed on a resume, to another set at a new univer-

---

125 See, again, the already cited study *Moral Mazes* by Robert Jackall.

sity. If propaganda is management, and if administrators manage, then administrators propagandize. Everybody does it, but it is not admitted to in polite society. The squeamishness here is Victorian in scope.

Propagandists are therefore prodigious pseudomorphs. Titles under which propagandists may do their work are not only legion, but often very creative. An offhand few include: public relations; community relations; government relations; public information; publicity; media relations; publicist; speechwriter, reporter; communication(s) specialist, technician or sometimes just plain communication(s); human relations and diversity; communication consultant; public affairs; development officer; marketing; donor relations; editor; counselor; campaign manager; public diplomacy; cultural affairs; human resources director; managers and directors of many sorts; and of course all varieties of terms involving the word education. And let's not forget "community organizer." Propaganda finds a way and a suitably ambiguous title.

Huge administrative propaganda machines may operate under euphemistic pretenses. At its peak, for example, in its nearly half-century of official existence, the United States Information Agency employed several thousand persons, mainly for "informing" people in foreign countries (especially in the Soviet bloc) via news, education and entertainment broadcasts. To my knowledge, not one of these propagandists was ever officially titled a "propagandist." As early as 1913, the U.S. Congress had become sensitized to the practice of government bureaucracies creating favorable news to manipulate public opinion at taxpayer expense. This was ethically problematic because taxpayer funds were as a directly being used to promote the careers of the same officials who were spending them. Congress specifically banned the use of budgeted funds for publicity experts. This stopgap was and remains a lost cause. The result was merely that different job titles were substituted for identical functions, many so ambiguous as to defy any attempt to pin them down functionally. And today, jaded by a lifetime of exposure to propaganda, few even bother to question the imperial scale on which modern White House communication operates from day-to-day; each day is a re-election campaign.

In an apparent ethical paradox, the term *propaganda* sees use in modern professional propaganda almost exclusively as an ethical indictment. Although organizations may conduct propaganda tirelessly under benign labels, the term itself is only directed at opponents who must be discredited. When our side does it, it is "educating the public" or the consumer, and when those over yonder do it, especially those whom we dislike, it becomes "propaganda." I heard a professor at the University of Michigan, upset over the content of a student's persuasive speech, denounce it as "propaganda," because the student expressed rather popular conservative views on why Ronald Reagan was a great man. The same professor, however, routinely spoke in the standardized leftist language of "critical theory," e.g., struggle, hegemony and praxis, with which she saw no association whatsoever with propaganda. She believed this even though critical theory as taught in universities is a Marxist-derived intellectualist propaganda that, among other things, purportedly provides an analytic tool to understand capitalist system propaganda. This would be rather funny if it were not for the fact that critical theory is advocated so earnestly by so many naïve, propagandizing academics. Even though this professor taught persuasion and might reasonably be presumed an expert, she could see nothing beyond her nose, and only in the manner in which she had been trained.

Ethical posturing is intrinsic to either side of the propaganda divide — with propagandists behaving as ethical justifiers, and the social critics denigrating propaganda on ethical grounds. The famous Aristotelian definition of Man as the "political animal" should perhaps be enlarged to "the ethically posturing political animal." The whole idea of propaganda plays strongly in attempts to realize the human need to be seen as in-the- right by oneself and others.[126]

Ethos Almighty

When Aristotle systematized the art of rhetoric he identified *ethos* as one of the most heavily weighted factors in persuasion. All else being equal, the source with good ethos prevails. This is true also for propaganda, which differs from classical persuasion in being more impersonal and mass-produced with standardization in mind. Ethos refers

---

126 See Stanley Cunningham's *The Idea of Propaganda: A Reconstruction* (Westport, CT: Praeger Publishing, 2002). In addition to thoroughly reviewing the intellectual history of propaganda, Professor Cunningham, professor emeritus at the University of Windsor, Ontario, has much to say on the ethics of propaganda, which he regards as a form of non-communication. He is like Ellul, in designating propaganda as necessarily evil because of its effects and intentions. This is a far-seeing work, the culmination of a lifetime of serious scholarship.

to ethics, as in the practiced or apparent virtues. It is often translated as "credibility," which is not quite right, however, because credibility is the product of a good ethos.

A source with perceived good ethos is innately persuasive. The truly good man or woman is a powerful person in terms of social effects. The good have impact. For is it not true that one tends to believe and follow the word and example of those whom one trusts? We trust the good, as we should. Often we lack direct substantive information concerning the matters at hand and have only our trust in the assurances of these others to go on.

We rely on ethos and its signs, which are many, although not infallible. Propagandists regularly ape them. There are probably too many signs to comprehensively list, but a high-ethos person is well-intentioned, fair, honest and forthright, looks you in the eye and gives a good handshake. Even if this person happens to be not-so-well-spoken, he is innately more believable than an apparently evil person, the bad man with bad ethos, the character who is not believable even if he may provide a better argument, be more superficially attractive, or is slicker in his appeals. The wise person may date based on looks, but marries based on ethos. Everyone knows some big-talking acquaintance always filled with schemes, all hat and no cattle, touting the prospects of imaginary empire, for which he wants support either financially or otherwise. Big talk aside, and despite any proofs offered, you know in your heart that you would be more likely to recover your investment if you threw your money out the window of your car while driving down the expressway. Losers, cheats, braggarts, hypocrites, bigamists, bullies and liars have low ethos.

Those who are crabbed and negative also fail at ethos. A sure way to marginalization in any organization is to go about always complaining or viciously gossiping. This is why in political campaigns it is common practice to divvy up the positive and negative parts of the undertaking. The candidate must appear a positive force and, as prearranged, confines remarks to policy and matters of greatness. Meanwhile negative attacks are conducted by someone else in the party — someone once or twice removed from the candidate, or, especially effective, by a front organization that produces attack ads, media events such as protests and rumor-mongering (see Commandment Six). In this way, the campaign has the best of both worlds — a coordinated positive image and vicious attack.

Generally speaking, other ways of compromising ethos include any conspicuous loss of emotional control such as public displays of anger, obvious unhappiness, instability, intransigency, questionable associations and crazy family members. Exaggerated talk, hyperbole, will also do it. Generally speaking, ethos flows from moderation, circumspect talk appropriate to the social role of the source and expectations of the occasion, common sense, benign intent, success, hard work or its appearance, consistency, faithfulness, similarity in looks and background with the target audience and appropriate dress. Good looks matter, as does the appearance of robust health. Too skinny, too fat, dressed like a bum, run down at the heels — forget it, at least for most audiences most of the time. Look for models to salespeople in successful outlets. Circumstantial exceptions exist, although are fewer than might be thought, which is why propaganda is an art and not merely a collection of recipes.

There are also wispy but far-from-intangible factors such as charm or charisma, which some people seemingly exude naturally, some quite unnaturally, and which in others seem to operate in reverse. Ethos based on charisma alone may be sufficient to deeply persuade. Salt of the earth appeals are common, where the propagandist drapes his subject in the good old-fashioned, everyday virtues of the common folk. I talked to a woman who had once sat upon a U.S. Senator's knee, many, many years previous, whom she thought a fine fellow with a down-to-earth personality. Years later apparently on this basis alone, she voted for his son who was running for President. Many politicians have been gifted with a ready lowest-common-denominational sort of charm, sharing a channel with the folk, e.g., governors who dance at polka fests, another who used to sing "The Tennessee Waltz" at county fairs all over that state and Congressmen who show up at local sportsman clubs' wild game dinners to partake of the roast muskrat swimming in creamed corn.

Folksy charm can work. After having seen it applied so many times, campaign staff members may roll their eyes, but the people affected usually don't seem to notice. If people do notice, watch out. Wrath is incurred by the fake who is out to fool people, by the perceived attempt to deceive. Ivy League politicians who take off their ties and suit coats and roll up their sleeves to patronize working class audiences are taking a risk. But I talked with a farmer who was deeply impressed that a gubernatorial candidate got out of a car, walked across the fields, and introduced himself. The farmer, once off his tractor, became a walking political advertisement for the candidate, who won, to the complete surprise of his opponent's party that had been in power. I believe the win came because he projected ethos far better than his opponent, who during the campaign stayed closeted with fellow party members.[127] The personal touch goes a long way in establishing ethos. A person with good ethos can get away with almost anything — once.

Conspicuous displays of family values also effectively demonstrate ethos. The reason we see so many politicians and corporate leaders with their more presentable family members is because this simulates the ethos of the good family man/woman, just like you and me, or at least as we should like to be. Nowadays in this post-*Leave-it-to-Beaver* era, the politicians include their problem children too in these staged tableau scenes to illustrate that they too have domestic worries like everybody else. "I'm like you," is the message. Novelist Charles Dickens routinely used such heavy-handed tableaux to tie off his sentimental stories. Dickens' tableaux, however corny, uncannily resemble the crowded endings that have become common for televised political events such as the convention speech or debate, where the extended family, friends, political allies and Tiny Tim, too, or his substitute, cluster onstage around the leader in a grand set piece of schmaltzy ethos theatre. Even the current Presidential family's cat or dog sends a message of ethos to millions of animal lovers: anyone who loves animals must be good, whatever people may say, right?[128] The Clintons even dragged their animals along on vacations, apparently for the purpose of ethos-building media events; you may recall, though, how quickly they rid themselves of the once-celebrated White House cat upon leaving office.

Politicians are also great joiners: NRA, VFW, NAACP, Rotary, Masons, Knights of Columbus, etc. They try to exploit the influence of these groups, but mainly the purpose is to signal ethical similarities to key voting constituencies. They go to church, too, incessantly, accompanied by their families and the TV cameras.

---

127 I found myself between jobs during that election cycle and, with the help of personal contacts, approached the party of the incumbent (the one who eventually lost) to see if I might work for the campaign. I had very definite ideas about the need to get out and talk to people. The campaign manager rebuffed me, saying that they saw no reason to hire me as they had everything under control. I take my vengeance with this footnote.

128 Hitler had a dog.

Something as apparently straightforward as a State of the Union Address becomes a way of signifying ethos. Who sits with whom? Who is mentioned? In an ethos-enhancing show of fairness, the President almost invariably concedes that "the other side of the aisle" has some good ideas and "we" all need to work together. No follow-through is necessary, or seriously intended in all likelihood, for the purpose here is only to seem fair and reasonable, at no political cost whatsoever, the actual doing being an altogether unrelated matter. Don't overlook the big happy family tableaux pseudo-events now customarily broadcast at the end of the State of the Union and election nights.

Other ethos-enhancing techniques include legend-building processes for candidates and organizational leaders — the stage-managing of character and cults of leadership based on something called "vision." We find here the usual ghostwritten autobiographical manifestos. Oh, the glorious names given to these books and films! Some examples: *The Man from Hope, It Takes a Village,* a phrase that circulated in social service circles long before it was picked up for the book, *The Audacity of Hope, Going Rogue, Faith of my Fathers* and *Profiles in Courage,* which won a Pulitzer prize for John F. Kennedy, even though those in the know identify it as the work of speechwriter Theodore Sorenson.

Books constitute a prestige medium; a candidate without one is no candidate. It matters little if few people really read them — one wonders how many actually do — but people buy and brandish them as they are touted with magnificent efficiency on the talk show circuit. Nowadays such books are knocked out by publishers so fast as to defy comprehension (and by the way, I should have included "ghostwriter" in the list of titles for working propagandists).

Typical in the stage management of the ethical character, we see Abe Lincoln the rail-splitter in his Illinois backwoods cabin; Sarah Palin, fishing, moose-hunting ex-governor and soccer mother; and those two salt-of-the-earth Yale graduates, the previously mentioned Al Gore, Jr. on the farm pretending to chop wood, incongruously dressed in polo shirt and slacks, and George W. Bush on the ranch equally incongruous in denims and clodhoppers.

Private corporations often project ethos through architectural grandeur and what has been called institutional advertising — showing how their services tie together the global economy, ensure connectivity and knit the modern world into a consumer paradise where people are more productive than ever before — although at exactly *what* remains unstated. The audience member can fill in the blanks by projecting his fantasies and prior expectations. Or corporations show how they are fighting carbon emissions, poverty, world hunger (how does this differ from regular hunger?) and working to support sustainability, alternative energy and whatever else that current fashions in virtue may demand. After watching these advertisements, one could almost think these businesses operated as global charities. Corporations also demonstrate good "corporate citizenship," especially in communities where they operate facilities, by supporting local events and causes. In all this, though, private corporations are more or less straightforward — doing it because it is good for business. One knows what they are selling. If images of wolves, polar bears and unbelievably wholesome families happen to be used to sell it, the product is usually more or less innocuous, and one has the additional option of not buying in. People understand the game. Private corporations are broadly socially acceptable within well-proscribed limits, as they exist on the whole to make a profit, or for some specific purpose, and claim no power over anything other than that which is their own. Much more serious and pernicious is ethically based propaganda by public bureaucracies for large-scale, governmental social programs from which one cannot escape.

Interior Colonization

Ours may be the Saurian Age of public administrative bureaucracy, giant governmental organizations that shake the earth and blot out the sun as they lumber about. They proliferate in number and scope. Federal, state, county and municipal governments and agencies now extend into more spaces, physical and psychological, than ever before imaginable. Somewhere around six million people work full time for state and federal government in the U.S.[129] This figure does not include the many nonprofit and service agencies funded by and, hence, constrained by, the strings attached to public money doled out by government agencies. Administrative public bureaucracy claims power over the spectrum of human activities: conception, marriage, relationships between the sexes, birth and child rearing; education, K-12 and

---

129 The U.S. Census Bureau supports a web page with annual summaries broken down by function. See http://www.census.gov/govs/apes/.

beyond, even in private colleges that accept federal money in financial aid; taxation; work; play; psychological well-being; health, food and drugs; manufacturing and farming; real estate, natural resources, imports and exports; commerce; transportation; regulation of private corporations; communication and even aging and death.

This level of domination can only take place in a heavily ethicized atmosphere, otherwise it would be perceived as the arbitrary exercise of raw power. A natural output of this administrative bureaucracy, therefore, is ethics-based propaganda that justifies its existence and continued extension of power. Because mass democracy stands unchallenged as the modern ethical norm, legitimate power must claim to represent "all the people" without exclusions, especially those who cannot represent themselves — which appears to be an increasingly large group. Administration must appear open, transparent, efficacious, representative, efficient, fair, benign, diverse, responsive, rational, proactive, accountable, and deeply rooted in public service.

Further, the retrogressive cycle inherent in mass democratic politics places increasingly miraculous expectations on government, delivery of which at some point becomes impossible: the lame must not merely walk but run, the Malthusian-poor not only fed but supplied with nutritious meals rather than junk food, and the congenitally stupid or lazy not only educated, but graduated at university level in accelerated degree programs so as to somehow stimulate the economy. Returning to the discussion of scientism in the previous chapter, this amounts to mass magical thinking. Political parties buy votes with promises of magical solutions in matters of the problem-of-the-day. Not only must the impossible be done, it must appear to be done immediately, for next week attention will be focused on a different problem.

Administrative apparatchiks, whom experience has taught that perceptions of their work matter far more than tangible performance, stand and deliver accordingly. Another new vaporous program is rolled out, low on substance, high on ethical pretense: no child left behind, outcome-based education, the student-centered university and the academic journey. Be assured this list does not end here. Unadorned efficacy with a reasonable assurance of long-term results is propagandistically insufficient, even though it might provide a realistic schematic for development. Bureaucracies must constantly serve up propagandistic demonstrations of total service and representation. These are not merely facile efforts — as Princeton philosopher Harry Frankfurt observes in his fabulously titled monograph *On Bullshit* — this "carefully wrought bullshit" is frequently produced by "exquisitely sophisticated craftsmen,"[130] many of whom seem to believe it themselves.

Especially in education and human services, where the gap between needs and reality is probably the most abysmal, public administration thus becomes an apparatus for the purpose of purveying ethical visions. This, and not irksome substance, is where the payoff lies in terms of professional careers and leadership positions. While this may be long-term suicide, culturally speaking, especially in education, we live in a short-term society. The production of propaganda takes precedence. Organizational theorists call this substitution phenomenon "goal displacement."[131]

A last matter pertaining to the situation: my interpretation of modern history is that the West has moved from a period of exterior-directed colonization to one of interior-directed colonization. What I mean by this is that the Western expansionism as manifested by colonization, subjection of the world, its raw materials and new markets that began roughly about the 1400s, has reached its approximate natural limits. It is becoming increasingly obvious that we will not be colonizing outer space at any time soon, if at all.[132] The easy pickings are gone. There remain no dark, unexplored interiors of continents like America and Africa, where arable land, beaver pelts, gold nuggets or uranium could be had by the first comer, or bought outright from primitive inhabitants with a bolt of red cloth and some glass beads. Major portions of the formerly undeveloped world have developed and offer stiff competition for markets and resources. The old Western economies were driven by fresh natural resources processed into wealth by matchless industrialized economies that supplied wide open markets. Well, the Western economies aren't so matchless anymore.

The colonial impulse still lingers — a hermeneutic — along with associated habits of mind such as exploration, utilization, exploitation, belief in progress and hyper-rational bureaucratic organization. Following professional training and historical precedent, lacking other

---

130 Harry G. Frankfurt, *On Bullshit* (Princeton, NJ: Princeton University Press, 2005).

131 Robert Michels, who also introduced the Iron Rule of Oligarchy, based on his case study, which explains how a supposedly democratic open organization — ironically the social democratic political party in Germany — turned quickly into an autocratic group that only maintained the appearance of participation.

132 As the jape goes, "No space travel for this generation."

outlets, and following the path of least resistance, the Western habit of colonization has turned inward. The trend for quite some time has been toward interior colonization. We now have something euphemistically called a service economy. Interior colonization is the administrative mapping, organization, management and development of its own people in just about every dimension possible — the human services industry. And then make the humans pay the bill. Administrative classes herd, sort, catalog and service, inscribing new power relationships. The atomized masses are every bit as exploitable as a vein of gold, actually more so, for while gold is only where you find it, and always in limited supply, social needs are both ubiquitous and exponentially self-renewing. The public administrative bureaucracies represent the modern frontier for forward-thinking propagandists.

Projecting the Ethos of Openness

Regarding propaganda techniques favored in public administration, one sees beside the repertoire discussed throughout this book, a focus on high-power, ethical significations, often with an emphasis on appearances of transparency and participation. Public bureaucracies usually excel at controlling the flow of information, as the First Commandment requires, while maintaining the illusion of openness.

Except perhaps at the lower levels of county and municipal government, public meetings of boards and regulatory bodies are routinely staged farces, directed by staff and leaders, where all has already been decided, sometimes by a nod and wink. The meeting itself functions as a fait accompli used for announcement purposes and demonstration of ideological solidarity, but not deliberation. The give and take of real democracy or even intelligent discussion is far too messy a business to hazard in public. Messiness creates bad press; competitors and critics may sense weaknesses. The administrative master plan must unroll smoothly at risk of attracting closer scrutiny than it can bear, and owing to the frequent preference for magical methodologies, cannot usually withstand all that much scrutiny.

Sunshine laws that apply to public administration, e.g., open meeting statutes and requests based on the Freedom of Information Act (FOIA), are routinely evaded depending on the power of the requester. Big media are feared, so cooperation with reporters is more likely, as with subpoenas, but individuals are often ignored or trifled with. Legal stipulations concerning FOIA compliance set limits on personnel actions, bids, client records, ongoing investigations and overly broad requests. Officials will deny a request as being too broad, or that no such specific record exists, even though the only way to know the exact title would be to already have a copy. I have also seen public officials deny the existence of documents such as contracts with consultants who were actively and visibly engaged in current business with the organization. Opportunities for equivocation are numerous. Even a supposedly simple black-and-white document such as the annual budget can be turned into a masterwork of obfuscation. A public university with which I am familiar went from the annual profit/loss balance sheet format, understandable at a glance, to a 60-page long online format that a Ph.D. in economics described as raising more questions than it answered. Funds just appeared and disappeared in seemingly ghostly fashion. Such obfuscation is deliberate. The administrative budget game appears much the same everywhere — there is always money for the current ruling clique's hobby horses, or for a new consultant's report, or the spin-off new technology project, but major cuts are needed elsewhere, even more next year. The only thing in the open about such matters is the constant play-acting.

A currently fashionable tactic for feigning the ethos of openness is the ersatz town hall meeting. This new style meeting has little in common with the old town hall meetings of New England. The latter were democratic discussions by townspeople who were coequals within a recognized forum of local government democracy. People, genuinely autonomous, debated arguments. They had their say. The ersatz town hall meeting is instead a highly controlled propaganda event that gives an appearance of open democratic participation without the accompanying inconvenience of actually having to play host or respond to unwelcome ideas. To augment the appearance of openness it is broadcast, or now, borrowing from the glory of the Internet as the global village, it is streamed live in online format and then preserved on the organizational web pages as an e-monument to openness. I heard of one recently that was also twittered, perhaps the height of trendy absurdity. The format generally features an organizational principal, maybe a CEO or president, usually accompanied by a sidekick PR functionary or guest who may read questions to the principal, who then provides communication in the top down sense. Questions come presumably from the audience, and may be submitted by email. The format is of course every bit as fake as a 1950s era game show. A series of pseudo-town halls that I observed were scheduled in a room too small to contain more than 20 or so people. The audience consisted of an entourage of members of the administrative team demonstrating their paid loyalty, and sometimes the same one or two crank employees who attended everything. There was no public. The questions were lobbed softballs, obviously submitted by administrative team members to allow the principal a chance to make a show of concerned knowledge. Sometimes a question would be handed over to the vice president of whatever department was concerned, or to a director of some new initiative, who just happened to be in the audience with a scripted response. An observer without considerable prior inside knowledge, however, watching from a distance, say online, or seeing an announcement of the meetings, would probably innocently presume honest, fair discussion. This ethos-enhancing format approaches near total control of information.

The same public organization abruptly added to its multi-million-dollar communication array all sorts of blogs and web pages on which select, co-opted persons (recipients of organizational favors) were invited to share their enthusiasm over administrative initiatives. This took up a great deal of bandwidth in organizational communication, replacing the need for newsletters, and having the additional advantage of appearing to casual observers as an open community at work and play. To my knowledge, no dissenters ever appeared in these hothouse media. An alternative blog set up beyond the reach of official authority was viciously attacked, its contributors slandered, but not officially, by friends of the administration who were later rewarded with jobs. Any such alternative views threaten not only interpretive monopoly, but also the all-important ethos of administrators. Things seemed open when they were anything but.

Another wonderfully effective means of open-seeming obfuscation is that now universally accepted form of pseudo-communication, the PowerPoint presentation, which has quickly became a standard skill taught in speech classes. Organizationally, however, it has grown into a time consuming practice that devours agenda time at public meetings by entraining them to 45-60 minute slide presentations. Instead of useful discussion — e.g., the questioning of assumptions — meetings become a linear progression from one slide to the next, with the patter of the speaker connecting disassociated representations, bullet points, graphs, Venn diagrams and multicolored flow charts. I witnessed one where a slide depicting a chipmunk was used to show how the organization could not "nibble away" at the budget. One later finds the slides posted on organizational websites and used to justify all sorts of arbitrary decisions. After eating up the available time, the trickster will then project a slide on which he has written his own set of "probing" questions, and for which he has carefully prepared responses. Having had this trick played on me, as a chair of academic committees, I have vowed never again to allow administrators to clog discussion agendas with such nonsense. Consultant Edward Tufte has observed that this "cognitive style of PowerPoint" really "reduces the analytic quality of presentations."[133] Which is exactly why the style is useful to administrators. They don't want deep analysis. They want nodding conformity and softball questions. Talk in some enlightened circles is of banning such presentations at meetings. Advantages accrue to the administrators in these matters, however.

Ethical codes of conduct, mission and vision statements elevate propagandistic activities to the level of the broader social service, cloaked in *public service* and *education*. Ethics empower propaganda.

In the service economy, propaganda becomes a work product much like anything else — only perhaps more liquid. The "let them eat cake" style is long passé these days. The contemporary style is "let them eat propaganda."

I sincerely hope for better than this from Western Culture.

---

133 See Edward R. Tufte, *The Cognitive Style of PowerPoint*, a short and excellent read.

APPENDICES

Appendix One: Definitions of Propaganda

I once collected about 30 definitions of *propaganda* before reaching a stage of diminishing returns. Only a few are presented here. My preferred *situational propaganda* or *informational sociology* approach — an approach, I say, instead of a narrow definition which restricts as much as it assists perception — is derived partly from Walter Lippmann's already quoted definition, and partly from observation, having been on the receiving end of much information doled out by self-serving elites and would-be elites. No doubt both definitions are influenced by Karl Marx's much quoted observation that the ruling ideas in any epoch are the ideas of the ruling classes. Leonard Doob, a Yale psychologist, in advising on the study of propaganda, avoided any single definition because the term represented such "a significant segment of behavior" that Doob thought a single definition was insufficient to cover the territory. See *Public Opinion and Propaganda* (North Haven, CT: Shoe String Press, 1966). Also I do not differentiate between a communication campaign and a propaganda campaign, except to note that modern planners prefer the more euphemistic term for obvious reasons, unless of course they are talking about the opposition.

Harold Lasswell used several definitions throughout his career: (1) "For analytical purposes ... anyone who uses representations to influence public opinions is a propagandist." To which he adds, "Propaganda in the United States is notable for its quantity and for the high degree of specialization that has arisen in connection with it." (2) In his earliest work he defines it as "....the control of opinion by significant symbols, or, to speak more concretely and less academically, by stories, rumors, reports, pictures, and other forms of social conversation (1927, 9). (3) Also: "Propaganda in the broadest sense is the technique of influencing human action by the manipulation of representations" (*Encyclopedia of the Social Sciences,* Edwin R. A. Seligman (Ed.), (London: Macmillan, 1934).

The Oxford English Dictionary, probably an as authoritative source as exists on the historical development of the English language, defines propaganda as: "Any association, systematic scheme or concerted movement for the propagation of a particular doctrine or practice."

Jowett and O'Donnell, authors of *Propaganda and Persuasion* (Thousand Oaks, CA: Sage Publications, 2012), a text often used in persuasion/propaganda classes, state, "Propaganda is the deliberate and systematic attempt to shape perceptions, manipulate cognitions, and direct behavior to achieve a response that furthers the desired intent of the propagandist." How this may differ from education, social work, parenting, pastoral care, business management, marketing, marriage or evangelism, I am uncertain.

One of my favorite propaganda definitions comes from anthropologist Clifford Geertz: "(1) a system of symbols which acts to (2) establish powerful, pervasive, and long-lasting moods and motivations in men by (3) formulating conceptions of a general order of existence and (4) cloaking these conceptions in an aura of factuality that (5) the moods and motivations seem uniquely realistic" ("Religion as a Cultural System," *Anthropological Approaches to the Study of Religion,* (London: Tavistock, 1985), XLIII, p. 176). Unfortunately after reading the definition, I discovered that Geertz was actually trying to define *religion,* but I find it serves very well for propaganda too because it includes the desired totalitarian effects. Religion and propaganda thrive in much the same soil.

Pratkanis and Aronson in their fairly popular text define it as: "Mass suggestion of influence through the manipulation of symbols and the psychology of the individual, often through lies and deceptions." This perhaps overly dramatic definition well reflects the popular American use of the term. See *Age of Propaganda: Everyday Uses and Abuses of Persuasion* (New York: Holt Paperbacks, 2001).

Deep-thinking Jacques Ellul defines a number of subtypes of propaganda. These include: *Vertical* — the traditional top down sort associated with organizational pronouncements; *Horizontal,* which employs small groups to help its subjects mold their own behavior through conformity; *Sociological,* of the sort that conveys cultural values and is often spread via entertainment and cultural productions, e.g., the People's Republic of China is currently trying to set up "Confucius Institutes" in U.S. universities; *Political*, which serves the needs of identifiable political parties-entities; *Agitation Propaganda*, or *agitprop*, which attempts to disintegrate an established order or value system; and *Integration*, the opposite of agitprop. To this we might add *Black Propaganda*, which is disinformation from a covert source; *White Propaganda*, where both source and message are overt; and *Grey Propaganda*, which is true, but where the source is hidden, as it is sometime advantageous for the sake of credibility for an actual source to remove itself from the scene.

Altheide and Johnson's distinction between traditional and bureaucratic propagandas illuminates much. *Traditional propaganda*, they say, is directed at a mass audience via channels of mass media propagandists by means of selected truths for the deliberate purpose of altering attitudes corresponding to the goals of the propagandist. *Bureaucratic propaganda*, however, is directed at selected audiences of influential people such as legislators and other budgetary evaluators, through media of specialized reporting and official communications such as hearings, testimony and committee reports that are "scientifically" contrived to resemble objective research methods, to satisfy these evaluators so as to justify and legitimate the propagandist's organization (and especially its continued funding). An example, taken from personal observation: a social service demonstration project printed 1,000 leaflets that were given to street people to pass out in the "target community." Even though most, if not all, leaflets appeared to have been discarded in dumpsters, the project administrators reported to their funding agency an additional 1,000 people served by the project based on the measure that each leaflet reaches, on average, one person and is therefore one "unit" of service. Altheide and Johnson's book of case studies, *Bureaucratic Propaganda* (Boston: Allyn & Bacon, 1980) has been under-appreciated.

Appendix Two: Horrors of the War

Ernst Jünger was a German officer who was wounded 14 times. He speaks of earth plowed by high-explosive shells that constantly uncovered the rotted remains of soldiers and horses lost in previous offensives; of the constant death-miasma of the front; of comrades decapitated by shell splinters; of rats and their ghastly diet; of being more than once upended by artillery shells that buried themselves at his feet without exploding; of the muscular knees of the still warm bodies of kilted Scotch Highlanders that he and his comrades climbed over while battling for terrain; all in all, four years of horror. On his experience of wartime propaganda he wrote:

> I found vast quantities of literature thrown down from aeroplanes. It was designed to hasten the moral deterioration of the army; among it was even Schiller's poem of Britannia the Free. It seemed very clever of the English to bombard us with poetry, and also very flattering to us. A war in which one fought with verses would indeed be a treat. The reward of thirty pfennigs set on the head of each copy by the military authorities showed that they did not undervalue the danger of this weapon. The cost of this, it is true, was laid upon the occupied territory. So it would appear we possessed no longer the wholly pure understanding of poetry.

Jünger also mentions storming a dugout and finding, "English newspapers that abounded in the most tasteless invective against the 'Huns.'"

From a broader view, Germany and her war partners lost five million soldiers killed outright in the war. Millions more on both sides were crippled, disfigured and blinded by poison gas (Adolf Hitler was in hospital recovering from being blinded in a gas attack when he learned of the Armistice). The British, in turn, bled out almost a whole generation of manhood, sometimes losing 20,000 men in a single day, a feat they repeated several times. Meanwhile their recruiting posters showed handsome women overlooking marching soldiers, captioned, "Women of Britain say — 'Go!'" At railway stations and other public places, groups of British women handed out white feathers symbolic of cowardice to men who appeared of military age but were not in uniform.

Appendix Three:
The Tone of World War One's
Anti-German Propaganda

The tone of propaganda in the Great War is well known to those who have studied propaganda. Regarding the wave of anti-Germanism that sprung up at the time, in Montana Amish-like religious communitarians called Hutterites (locally known as "Hoots") moved *en masse* to Canada not to return until the 1950s and 1960s; they had espoused pacifism and spoke the German dialect *Schwäbisch*. An old man of German ancestry I knew when I was a teenager told me of his elementary schooling during this era. He was often beaten up and taunted by his schoolmates for his accent, name and heritage — treatment which he said had affected him for the rest of his life.

Contemporaneous "histories" convey what seems to have been the tone of the time — indictment. And I use "histories" in quotes, for although these books carried the weight of scholarship and authority, they now read as heavy-handed propaganda tracts. One example should suffice, taken from *King's Complete History of the World War* (Springfield, MA: The History Associates, 1922). This "impartial" history, intended for "the American people and youth of the Public Schools," commences with the following set of chapter headings:

HOW GERMANY LOST HER SOUL

Once an Inspired and Honored Member of the Exalted Family of Nations She Fell from Grace Through the Seductions of Prussian Paganism. Germany's Spiritual Surrender the Supreme Ethnic Tragedy of the Centuries. Prussian Barbarism Traced from its source in the Land of Gog and Magog. For 1300 years the Prussians Resisted the Influence of Christian Civilization. The Last Tribe in Europe to Abandon the Worship of Their Pagan Gods. Prussia's Duplicity, Treachery, and Her Evil Ambition to Govern the World. Prussian Principles of Government Absolutely Opposed to Human Liberty. Spiritual; Betrayal of Germany, The First step in Prussianization of the Planet. Corruption of the German Mind by Atheistic Philosophers and Historians. Blasphemous Teachings of Hegel, Fichte, Schlegel, Nietzsche, Trietzsche, Bernhardi. Germany Finally Renounces Her Christian Ideas, Reverting to Pagan Savagery. Prussia's Diabolical Plot

to Exterminate Christianity Throughout the World and Restore Their
Ancient Pagan Worship of Odin and Thor Universally.

The question that all this nonsense begs, all with a grain or more of
truth behind it, concerns the difference between history and propaganda. I will try to answer it in this way. History as employed in propaganda has little or nothing to do with the past, but everything to
do with the future. The propagandist explains the past so as to try to
control the future.

Appendix Four:
Hitler the Uni-Baller and Other
Propaganda Successes

A good portion of a generation of American men seemed to believe that Hitler had only one testicle, a pervasive rumor, rumor being yet another tool of propaganda. The British had a song, "Hitler has only got One Ball" which included the lyric "Himmler was similar." The implication was of an unnatural man whose motives, and whose very spirit, were blighted. It calls forth a deep cultural stereotype, a man injured in "'the stones" cannot be admitted to the Kingdom of Heaven, so says Scripture; the term "testimony" is said to arise from the act of a man placing his hand on his testicles and swearing by them. In the seventeenth century Francis Bacon in his *Essays* said of deformed persons, "For as Nature hath done ill by them, so doe they by Nature." If one considers the nature of Hitler and his acts, it makes no difference whatever whether he had one, two or a cluster of testicles. But propaganda must explain absolutely with no loose ends. Ambiguity is its enemy.

Regarding propagandistic ammunition that could have been used against Hitler and the Nazis, don't forget that the Holocaust was not really understood to have happened until war's end, in 1945 and later, so this information was not really available. Anti-Semitism was a common value of the time, in America and especially Europe, so the Nazi's anti-Semitism would probably not have made all that much impression on most mass audiences before the end of the war. Even famous Americans like Henry Ford publicly avowed, and in Ford's case actually promulgated, anti-Semitism. As always, the propagandists worked with what symbolic material was at hand: rumor, ridicule, the overdone militarism and the fascist's apparent disregard of the little guy.

If one considers in cold blood the matter of who were the better and bigger propagandists of World War II, however, Churchill and FDR proved the most effective (they won). American propaganda machinery was, and probably remains, the best in the world. While the Nazis had a state-controlled media system and functionaries like Fritz Hippler, who directed the turgid propaganda-documentary *The Eternal Jew,* America had Hollywood film geniuses such as Frank

Capra — who reassembled images taken from enemy propaganda and cultural films and used them to show why America simply had to fight. Capra, taking just one example from his wartime work, brilliantly juxtaposed sound and film clippings into an unforgettable scene from *Know Your Enemy: Japan.* The scene used film and sound of an industrial iron forge alternating with health, education and physical fitness film footage lifted from various Japanese productions, to show how the Japanese educational system burned the humanity out of children to produce its ultimate product, the Japanese soldier, ready to burn and slash his way across the world, so it was explained in the film. Next time you watch his *It's a Wonderful Life* on late night television during the holidays, consider that Capra was a propaganda genius because the very same set of empathies that made him a successful popular filmmaker assured that his propaganda films would work on their intended audience, too.

Capra (and Charlie Chaplin and even the Three Stooges) also recognized the considerable vulnerability of Hitler and the Nazis to pure mockery. An astonishing British short film of the war is called "The Lambeth Walk." It can be found online. Using rather clever editing techniques (for 1942) this two-minute propaganda masterpiece features cleverly edited film footage of Nazi storm troopers that appear to be doing chorus-line-style dance steps to a particularly mindless show tune of the era, "The Lambeth Walk." It delighted movie audiences in the U.S. and Britain, and was a great morale builder. It allegedly enraged Joseph Goebbels. Possibly the most astonishing aspect of this film, however, is that it was a British response to having been heavily bombed in what has since become known as the Battle of Britain, a series of air raids in which 30,000 British civilians were killed in London and elsewhere.

Acknowledgements

This book grew out of an undergraduate directed study more than twenty years ago at the University of Detroit under the auspices of Professors Vivian Dicks and George W. Pickering. The idea at the time was to further my decidedly unsystematic fascination with propaganda by: (1) compiling some sort of systematically organized bibliography/commentary on propaganda and (2) to have it published somewhere.

Propaganda was too big for me. Despite big ambitions, I could neither encompass it nor bring it down. I managed only a good beginning, discovering astonishing works by authorities on propaganda technique that hadn't been checked out of the library stacks since the 1950s, much of which seemed like forgotten knowledge of ancient sages.

I kept at it in my brooding way, an interest that sustained me through professional employment as a propagandist, graduate school at the University of Michigan and beyond. The reason why I teach propaganda in a Communication Department today is because no university has a Department of Propaganda, at least not yet, at least not in name. This book, then, represents not only the fulfillment of old agreements, but also the continuation (from my end) of a series of conversations with delightful people. I formally thank and acknowledge: Cindy Cantrell, David M. Cantrell, Bill Castanier, Stanley Cunningham, James Hill, Richard J. Knecht, J. Henry Lievens, John Black Morgan IV, Gillian Osswald, Tom Osswald, J.M. Sproule, Trevor Thrall, and David Tucker.

INDEX

Other books published by Arktos:

Beyond Human Rights
by Alain de Benoist

The Saga of the Aryan Race volumes 1-2
by Porus Homi Havewala

Manifesto for a European Renaissance
by Alain de Benoist & Charles Champetier

The Saga of the Aryan Race volumes 3-5
by Porus Homi Havewala

The Problem of Democracy
by Alain de Benoist

The Owls of Afrasiab
by Lars Holger Holm

Germany's Third Empire
by Arthur Moeller van den Bruck

De Naturae Natura
by Alexander Jacob

The Arctic Home in the Vedas
by Bal Gangadhar Tilak

Fighting for the Essence
by Pierre Krebs

Revolution from Above
by Kerry Bolton

Can Life Prevail?
by Pentti Linkola

The Fourth Political Theory
by Alexander Dugin

A Handbook of Traditional Living
by Raido

Metaphysics of War
by Julius Evola

The Agni and the Ecstasy
by Steven J. Rosen

The Path of Cinnabar:
An Intellectual Autobiography
by Julius Evola

The Jedi in the Lotus:
Star Wars and the Hindu Tradition
by Steven J. Rosen

Archeofuturism
by Guillaume Faye

It Cannot Be Stormed
by Ernst von Salomon

Convergence of Catastrophes
by Guillaume Faye

Tradition & Revolution
by Troy Southgate

Why We Fight
by Guillaume Faye

Against Democracy and Equality
by Tomislav Sunic

The WASP Question
by Andrew Fraser

The Initiate: Journal of Traditional Studies
by David J. Wingfield (ed.)

War and Democracy
by Paul Gottfried